BUILDING
VOCABULARY
SKILLS & STRATEGIES

LEVEL
3

by JOANNE SUTER

BUILDING VOCABULARY
SKILLS & STRATEGIES

LEVEL **3** ⇐

LEVEL **4**

LEVEL **5**

LEVEL **6**

LEVEL **7**

LEVEL **8**

Development and Production: Laurel Associates, Inc.
Cover Design: Image Quest, Inc.

SADDLEBACK
PUBLISHING·INC.

Three Watson
Irvine, CA 92618-2767

E-Mail: info@sdlback.com
Website: www.sdlback.com

ISBN 1-56254-721-6

Printed in the United States of America
10 09 08 07 06 05 04   9 8 7 6 5 4 3 2 1

CONTENTS

Welcome to
BUILDING VOCABULARY SKILLS & STRATEGIES!

We at Saddleback Publishing, Inc. are proud to introduce this important supplement to your basal language arts curriculum. Our goal in creating this series was twofold: to help on-level and below-level students build their "word power" in short incremental lessons, and to provide you, the teacher, with maximum flexibility in deciding when and how to assign these exercises.

All lessons are reproducible. That makes them ideal for homework, extra credit assignments, cooperative learning groups, or focused drill practice for selected ESL or remedial students. A quick review of the book's Table of Contents will enable you to individualize instruction according to the varied needs of your students.

Correlated to the latest research and current language arts standards in most states, the instructional design of *Building Vocabulary Skills & Strategies* is unusually comprehensive for a supplementary program. All important concepts—ranging from primary-level phonics to the nuances of connotation— are thoroughly presented from the ground up. Traditional word attack strategies and "getting meaning from context clues" are dually emphasized.

As all educators know, assessment and evaluation of student understanding and skill attainment is an ongoing process. Here again, reproducible lessons are ideal in that they can be used for both pre- and post-testing. We further suggest that you utilize the blank back of every copied worksheet for extra reinforcement of that lesson's vocabulary; spelling tests or short writing assignments are two obvious options. You can use the Scope and Sequence chart at the back of each book for recording your ongoing evaluations.

The meaning of a word is called its *definition.*

whale	feather	slight	vault

- A *whale* is a very large sea mammal.

- A *feather* is one of the soft, light parts that grow out of the skin of birds.

- Something *slight* is small in amount, strength, or importance.

- To *slight* something is to pay little or no attention to it.

- A *vault* is a room or special place for keeping valuable things.

- To *vault* is to jump over something.

Directions: Use the definitions to decide if each sentence below is true or false. If the sentence is *true*, write **T** on the line. If the sentence is *false*, write **F**.

1. _____ A whale is likely to be found swimming in the sea.

2. _____ Banks often lock money in a vault.

3. _____ If you vault a fence, you'll end up on the other side.

4. _____ A feather on a bird is somewhat like a hair on a dog.

5. _____ Even the biggest whale is very slight in size.

6. _____ A one-degree drop in temperature would be a slight change.

7. _____ If students slight their homework, they might not pass their tests.

Name: _____   **Date:** _____

You can be a poet! Just use the definitions to make the sentence pairs rhyme.

chore	hero	knob	dozen	hum

- A *chore* is a task that must be done.

- A *hero* is someone who is admired for doing something great or brave.

- A *knob* is a handle that is usually round.

- A *dozen* is a group of twelve.

- To *hum* is to sing with the lips closed, not saying the words.

Directions: Complete the rhymes. Choose one of the **boldface** words above. Write it on the blank line.

1. The knock at the door is Uncle Bob!
   He can come right in if he turns the _____.

2. The soccer score was one to zero.
   Then Mike scored a goal and was the team's _____.

3. Making the bed can be a real bore.
   Nonetheless, it's your daily _____.

4. While you sing along, my guitar I'll strum.
   If you don't know the words, why don't you just _____?

5. At the dinner table sat my aunt and cousin.
   Plus the ten in my family, that made a _____.

Name: _____   **Date:** _____

Synonyms are words that have the same or nearly the same meaning. Recognizing and using synonyms helps you build your vocabulary.

Directions: Circle the synonym for each **boldface** word.

1. The meat looked red and **uncooked**.

   (delicious / raw)

2. Maria told the dentist she had a **pain** in her tooth.

   (ache / hole)

3. I don't like cherry candy, so I'll **trade** this one for lime.

   (exchange / sell)

4. We watched the waves from the sandy **beach**.   (shore / desert)

5. The museum is **normally** closed on Tuesdays.   (seldom / usually)

6. The teachers expect **students** to arrive on time.   (pupils / buses)

7. Randy is **almost** as tall as his brother.   (exactly / nearly)

8. Sally tells her secrets to her **friend** Anna.   (sister / pal)

9. She also writes her secrets in a **diary**.   (journal / newspaper)

10. A tunnel led from the **basement** to the garage.   (cellar / barn)

11. The tunnel had a **concealed** entrance.   (hidden / open)

12. Don't drink from a cup if the **edge** is chipped.   (rim / glass)

Name: _____   **Date:** _____

> Use your wits to come up with the *synonyms* you
> need to correctly complete this page.

A. **Directions:** After each sentence, write a synonym for the **boldface**
word. The synonym should begin with the letter *g*.

EXAMPLE: The **huge** oak tree has grown here for years. ___*giant*___

1. The birthday **present** was wrapped in red paper. _____

2. Mr. Ramon will **donate** blood to the Red Cross. _____

3. The dog barks to **protect** his master's house. _____

4. The farmers were **happy** when the rain finally came. _____

B. **Directions:** On each blank line, write a
synonym for the **boldface**
word. The synonym should
begin with the letter *p*.

EXAMPLE: The **drawing** showed
a woman on a sailboat.

___*picture*___

1. Each **section** of the wall was a different color. _____

2. The workers dug a big **hole** in the field. _____

3. The **bundle** of paper was tied with string. _____

4. The farmer's prize **hog** won a ribbon at the fair. _____

Name: _____   **Date:** _____

Synonyms often add interest and variety to a story.

Directions: Read the story. Then match the **boldface** words with their *synonyms* (words with the same or nearly the same meaning).

Is Today the Day?

Brenda and her new husband, Bart, were out for a **walk** on a **cold** winter day. They walked past the **white** building that was the county animal shelter.

"Do you want to go in and see the dogs?" Brenda asked.

"Sure," Bart **answered**, "but today is not the day to take one home! Remember, we decided to wait until summer to get a **dog**!"

Inside the shelter, a worker led Brenda and Bart down the hall to the dog kennel. They were greeted by many hopeful barks that were clearly saying, "Take me home!"

Then Brenda saw a **strong**, black and tan dog with its nose pressed against the gate. It won her heart. Both the dog and Brenda looked at Bart with big, **excited** eyes.

Maybe the time was right after all!

pup	eager	ivory	frosty	powerful	stroll	replied

1. _____ is a synonym for *walk*.

2. _____ is a synonym for *cold*.

3. _____ is a synonym for *white*.

4. _____ is a synonym for *answered*.

5. _____ is a synonym for *dog*.

6. _____ is a synonym for *strong*.

7. _____ is a synonym for *excited*.

Name: _____   **Date:** _____

To make your vocabulary grow, practice working with these words to know!

Directions: First, complete the sentences with words from the box. Then complete the puzzle with the same words. Write one letter on each line. The answer to the riddle will read from top to bottom.

WORDS TO KNOW

exchange	frosty	hum	ivory	journal	stroll	witness

Riddle: *You might call me a "twin" because I am so much like another word. What am I?*

1. After dinner, it's nice to take a slow _____ around the block.

2. Some of the piano's 88 keys were black and others were _____ .

3. You can keep the sweater or _____ it for a larger size.

4. Juana wrote about daily events in her _____ .

5. Angela would testify in court as a _____ for the defense.

6. As autumn turned to winter, the mornings became cold and _____ .

7. Everyone else knew the words to the song, but I had to _____ along.

SOLUTION: *I am a*

1. __ __ __ __ __ __

2. __ __ __ __ __ __

3. __ __ __ __ __ __ __

4. __ __ __ __ __ __

5. __ __ __ __ __ __

6. __ __ __

7. __ __ __

Name: _____   **Date:** _____

Using the words in this exercise can help you answer *when* and *where* questions.

Directions: Replace the **boldface** words in the sentences with a word from the box. Write the new words on the blank lines.

WORDS THAT TELL "WHEN"
always   never   promptly   rarely   usually

1. **On very few days** _____ do I choose to eat my mother's meat loaf.

2. Mom **almost always** _____ cooks meat until it's as tough as leather.

3. When she's not looking, I **swiftly** _____ feed the meat loaf to our dog Barkly.

4. The dog has **at no time** _____ turned down meat.

5. **Every time** _____, Barkly drools and begs for more.

WORDS THAT TELL "WHERE"
among   beside   distant   inside   neighboring

6. Mirror Lake Mall, a wonderful shopping center, was built in a **nearby** _____ city.

7. The center is **right next to** _____ the lake, so shoppers can enjoy the view.

8. People come from **faraway** _____ places to shop at this mall.

9. You'll find a wonderful pizza restaurant **surrounded by** _____ gift shops, booksellers, and department stores.

10. When it's chilly outdoors, it's always warm and cozy **within the mall** _____.

Name: _____   **Date:** _____

Directions: Write a sentence that answers each question. Use one of the *where* and *when* words below in each sentence.

WHEN WORDS	WHERE WORDS
after	near
never	distant
seldom	above
regularly	beneath

1. What do you do when the school day is over?

_____

_____

2. What is something you do only on rare occasions?

_____

_____

3. What is something you do each and every day?

_____

4. What is something you always *avoid* doing in the classroom?

_____

5. What interesting building is close to your school?

_____

6. What relative lives the farthest from you?

_____

7. If you look up right now, what do you see?

_____

8. If you look down right now, what do you see?

_____

Name: _____ **Date:** _____

Many words have more than one meaning. The sound a bell makes is a *ring*. So is the band of jewelry you wear on your finger.

Directions: Draw a picture in each box to illustrate the meaning of the **boldface** word.

1. a. A black **bat** is hunting for insects at night in a garden.

    b. Frank hit a home run with a swing of his new **bat**.

2. a. I read a thrilling mystery **story** about a jewel thief.

    b. We had a grand view from our 12th-**story** apartment.

3. a. The **base** of the triangle is three inches long.

    b. The noisy jet took off from the Air Force **base**.

4. a. At $.50 a **pound**, peaches were a bargain today.

    b. **Pound** the nails straight into the board, or the wood might crack.

Challenge: Show another meaning for the word *base*. Draw a picture on the back of this sheet.

Name: _____   **Date:** _____

You may be surprised to find so many words with more than one meaning. Here are more multiple-meaning words for you to think about.

Directions: Look at the **boldface** word on the left. Then circle *two* letters on the right to show two different meanings of the word.

EXAMPLE: **peak**   (a.) the pointed top of a mountain or hill
               b.   a soft, yellow fruit
               (c.) the highest point or degree
               d.   a gift

1. **pool**
   a. a small pond
   b. a loud noise
   c. a small horse
   d. things shared by a group

2. **clump**
   a. to move by pushing
   b. a group of things growing close together
   c. to walk with a dull, heavy sound
   d. something long and narrow

3. **toast**
   a. a statement of praise or good wishes, usually given before drinking something
   b. warmed, browned bread
   c. a muscle found in the upper arm
   d. a loud, hearty laugh

4. **current**
   a. a prize given in return for hard work
   b. up to date, of the present time
   c. wet and slippery
   d. a flow of something such as air, water, or electricity

Challenge: Think of a word that has all the following meanings. Write it on the line. _____

- a series of musical notes from the lowest to the highest
- one of the thin, flat plates that cover and protect a fish's body
- a device or machine used for measuring weight
- to climb up

Name: _____ **Date:** _____

This story will give you more practice with words that have multiple meanings.

Directions: Read the story. Then write the **boldface** words on the lines next to their meanings.

Moving Day

It was moving day. Lulu and Lyle Lerner had **boxed** up most of their belongings. They were all **set** to move to their new house on the Pacific **coast**.

"After I load the TV **set** onto the truck, we can take off," Lyle said. He struggled to keep from dropping the heavy television on the **ground**. But Lyle was strong enough! He had **boxed** professionally for many years.

"Oh, no!" Lulu cried out. "Someone has parked a car in front of our truck. We're **boxed** in and can't get out!"

Luckily, the driver soon arrived to move the car. Then the Lerners piled into the truck.

"Our **gear** is all aboard now!" Lyle exclaimed. He **ground** the stick shift into first **gear** and began to **coast** down the driveway. "We're off to our new home!"

1. _____ means the land along the sea *or* to move without using power or effort

2. _____ means ready, prepared *or* a group of things that go together

3. _____ means a machine part made of wheels with teeth that fit together *or* belongings, tools, and equipment

4. _____ means the surface of the earth *or* rubbed together with a harsh, grating sound

5. _____ means packaged in a square, cardboard container *or* shut in, trapped *or* fought with one's fists as a sport

Name: _____   **Date:** _____

Read each word of the sentence carefully to see which meaning is intended.

Directions: Study each pair of sentences. Then write the multiple-meaning word from the box that matches both sentences.

case	drawing	fly	match	tie

1. The score was one to one.
   The band of cloth goes around his neck.

   These things are both a _____.

2. The ball was caught before it touched the ground.
   The black bug is a spider's favorite meal.

   These things are both a _____.

3. The picture was made with a pencil.
   The ticket was chosen and the winner announced.

   These things are both a _____.

4. I scratched this and it burst into flame.
   The blue scarf and blue sweater go together.

   These things are both a _____.

5. She has a bag for carrying things from place to place.
   This is a matter to be decided in a court of law.

   These things are both a _____.

Challenge: Choose one of the multiple-meaning words from the box. Write two sentences. In each sentence, use the word with a different meaning.

_____

_____

Name: _____ **Date:** _____

Here's your chance to show what you've learned about multiple-meaning words.

Directions: Use the words from the previous four lessons to complete the story. Write a word from the box on each blank line. You will use each word twice.

bat	box	current	story

The Creature in the Bedroom

"Yikes!" Christina cried. "There's a **(1)**_____ flying around in my bedroom!"

Christina's sister Claire came dashing upstairs to the second **(2)**_____ of the house. She was waving a long, wooden softball **(3)**_____ above her head.

"I'll get it!" she cried out.

"Chase it into a corner," Christina called out to Claire. "We'll try to **(4)**_____ it in."

The creature flew into the corner of the room.

"Don't hurt it!" Christina cried. "Here! Maybe we can get it into this cardboard **(5)**_____. Then we can take the box outside and let it go."

Claire opened the bedroom window. A **(6)**_____ of air seemed to attract the bat's attention. In a moment, it gave a squeak and flew out of the room. The girls breathed a happy sigh of relief.

"I know! Our **(7)**_____ assignment in language arts class is to write about an exciting experience. Well, I'm going to be writing the **(8)**_____ of the creature in my bedroom!" Christina exclaimed.

Name: _____ **Date:** _____

Now have some fun using multiple-meaning words in sentences of your own!

Directions: Write two sentences for each **boldface** word below. Make sure the word has a different meaning in each sentence. (Use a dictionary if you need help.)

EXAMPLE: **wave**

　　a. _Bob wanted to **wave** goodbye to his friends._
　　b. _The surfer rode to shore on the big **wave**._

1. **charge**

　　a. _____
　　b. _____

2. **check**

　　a. _____
　　b. _____

3. **horn**

　　a. _____
　　b. _____

4. **mole**

　　a. _____
　　b. _____

5. **shed**

　　a. _____
　　b. _____

Name: _____　　**Date:** _____

> *Antonyms* are words that have *opposite* meanings. When you think about antonyms, you stretch your vocabulary.

Directions: Read each sentence. Then circle the antonym for the **boldface** word. Try to picture the new image created when you substitute the antonym.

1. People stared as the **new** car went by.

   a. flashy   c. expensive

   b. ancient   d. unusual

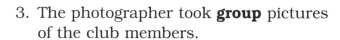

2. Damon, a great athlete, is **shorter** than most basketball stars.

   a. faster   c. taller

   b. stronger   d. heavier

3. The photographer took **group** pictures of the club members.

   a. individual   b. colorful   c. large   d. good

4. The north trail to the mountaintop is a very **safe** route.

   a. hard   b. long   c. risky   d. steep

5. Selma and Velma were twins who looked very **different**.

   a. similar   b. pretty   c. unusual   d. friendly

6. Large houses lined the **wide** street.

   a. winding   b. busy   c. shady   d. narrow

7. Near the end of the movie, I felt **sleepy**.

   a. bored   b. restless   c. sad   d. frightened

8. The child's tricks made his parents **grin**.

   a. laugh   b. angry   c. cry   d. frown

Challenge: Choose one of the sentences above. Illustrate what is happening. Then, draw what happens when you substitute the antonym for the **boldface** word. Draw your pictures on the back of this sheet.

Name: _____   **Date:** _____

What is the opposite of *same*? It's *opposite*! What is the antonym of *synonym*? It's *antonym*! If you understand those riddles, you're ready for this exercise!

Directions: The **boldface words** are *synonyms* (words that mean the same or nearly the same thing). Unscramble the **boldface letters** to spell an *antonym* for the boldface words.

1. If you're **hot**, you're **sizzling**!

   If you're not, you're (**DCLO**) _____.

2. If you're **close**, you're **near**.

   If you're distant, you're (**RFA**) _____.

3. If you're **foolish**, you're **silly**.

   If you're not, you're (**SEIW**) _____.

4. Your **future** is **tomorrow**.

   Yesterday is your (**STAP**) _____.

5. If you're **grown up**, you're **adult**.

   If you're not, you're a (**HILCD**) _____.

6. If you're **fearful**, you're **timid**.

   If you're not, you're (**DOLB**) _____.

7. If you're **tops**, you're the **best**.

   If you're not, you're the (**SWORT**) _____.

8. If you're **sick**, you're **ill**.

   If you're not, you're (**LEHATHY**) _____.

Name: _____   **Date:** _____

Synonyms **are words that mean the same or nearly the same thing.** *Antonyms* **are word pairs with opposite meanings.**

A. **Directions:** Tell whether each pair of words are *synonyms* or *antonyms*. Write **S** for *synonyms*. Write **A** for *antonyms*.

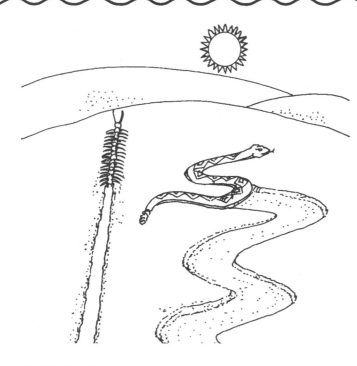

1. _____ follow / lead

2. _____ center / edge

3. _____ yelled / shouted

4. _____ scared / frightened

5. _____ admit / deny

6. _____ straight / zigzag

7. _____ break / repair

8. _____ tear / rip

9. _____ damp / moist

10. _____ clumsy / graceful

B. **Directions:** Now complete each sentence with one of the words listed above.

1. *Whispered* is an antonym for

   _____.

2. *Dry* is an antonym for

   _____.

3. *Awkward* is a synonym for

   _____.

4. *Crooked* is an antonym for

   _____.

5. *Afraid* is a synonym for

   _____.

6. *Fix* is a synonym for

   _____.

7. *Confess* is a synonym for

   _____.

8. *Middle* is a synonym for

   _____.

Name: _____   **Date:** _____

> You can often figure out the meaning of a new word by finding its *synonym* in the surrounding words.

Directions: Read each item. Then find and circle the synonym of the **boldface** word.

EXAMPLE: "Please put your **satchels** under the seat," said the bus driver. "We don't want people tripping over (bags)."

1. My **journey** began at the bus station. It would be the trip of a lifetime!

2. I pushed through the **throng**, hoping the crowd would not keep me from boarding my bus on time.

3. I didn't know that a great **ordeal**— a test of my strength—lay ahead.

4. Our bus had traveled about an hour when it entered a sand storm. **Grit** flew through the air.

5. "Stay in your seats!" the driver **urged**. He begged us to stay calm.

6. He was driving blind. **Sightless**, he bumped off the highway.

7. The bus ended up in a **gully**. The ditch was deep.

8. **Twilight** had fallen. In the dusk, we waited for help to come.

9. Hours passed. Some passengers felt **panic**. To ease their fear, I told jokes.

10. Some people praised my bravery. They said it took **courage** to keep a sense of humor in the face of danger.

Name: _____   **Date:** _____

You may find a pair of *antonyms* (words with opposite meanings) in some sentences. Understanding one antonym will help you figure out the meaning of the other word.

Directions: Read each item and notice the **boldface** word. Fill in the blank with a word from the box. The word you choose should be an *antonym* of the boldface word.

arose	exit	lively	polite	public	shallow	stale

1. Not **tired** enough for a nap, the _____ toddler ran about all day.

2. Scott is a _____ young man. He knows it would be **rude** to be late to the party.

3. At 5 P.M., the bakery gave away the _____ bread to make room for **fresh** loaves.

4. When the sun **set**, the moon _____ .

5. Don't go in that door! It's an _____ , not an **entrance**!

6. The Corner Cafe is usually open to the _____ , but today a **private** group has rented the space.

7. Young children should stay in the _____ end of the pool. **Deep** water can be dangerous.

Name: _____   Date: _____

Sometimes you'll find new words in a reading selection. The pictures or diagrams can help you figure out their meaning.

Directions: Read the selection. Look at the diagram. Then choose the answer to each question and circle its letter.

Tornadoes

It spins from the sky. It can lift a car and drop it miles away. It is one of the strongest storms known to man. It's a tornado!

Tornadoes usually occur in places that have a lot of thunderstorms. They often hit the center of the United States, which is known as the "Tornado Belt."

When a tornado forms, a dark wall cloud builds up under an anvil-shaped thundercloud. First rain and then hail may fall. Next a spinning cloud descends from the wall cloud to the ground. This "twister" is usually shaped like a funnel. It lifts rocks and even trees. The sound of things swirling in the air and crashing can sound like the roar of a freight train!

1. Where does a wall cloud build up?
   a. close to earth
   b. in the funnel
   c. under the anvil cloud

2. What types of moisture often come before a tornado?
   a. rain and hail
   b. hail and snow
   c. snow and sleet

3. What is the shape of a funnel?
   a. a column that is tall, narrow, and wider at the top
   b. a round and wide ball
   c. an even column that is the same width from top to bottom

4. In a tornado, which of the following touches the ground?
   a. the anvil
   b. the wall cloud
   c. the funnel

5. Why is the funnel called a "twister"?
   a. because it carries rain
   b. because it spins
   c. because it is dark

6. The funnel descends from the wall cloud. What does *descends* mean?
   a. rises from it
   b. spins around it
   c. moves downward from it

Name: _____   **Date:** _____

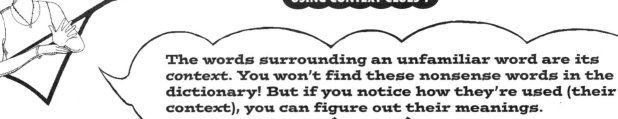

The words surrounding an unfamiliar word are its *context*. You won't find these nonsense words in the dictionary! But if you notice how they're used (their context), you can figure out their meanings.

Directions: Read each sentence and circle the nonsense word. Then, circle the letter of the word's meaning. (The only way to figure out the meaning is to use context clues.)

1. I think the Rodney Raccoon cartoon show is meant for codlinks rather than for adults.

   a. women   b. animals   c. children

2. Bridget washed her red, curly grawp every day to keep it shining and sweet-smelling.

   a. car   b. hair   c. apple

3. The pesky klampliver is digging holes in the yard and leaving hills and trails throughout the garden.

   a. mole   b. gardener   c. steam shovel

4. Because Mr. Parker missed the last fledlamk, he did not make it home in time for dinner.

   a. movie   b. baseball   c. bus

5. When Mr. Parker swung his bat and missed the fizmark, the umpire called "Strike One!"

   a. bus   b. baseball   c. table

6. Pumpkin pie, a delicious lorghat, is just perfect to finish off an autumn meal.

   a. dessert   b. beverage   c. apron

7. As the music played, Gerald took a breath, smiled, opened his mouth, and burst into qualtzmk.

   a. flames   b. tears   c. song

8. The mad wraxbuldman mixed chemicals in a test tube, drank them down, and began to laugh.

   a. mechanic   b. librarian   c. scientist

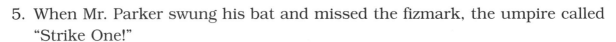

Name: _____   **Date:** _____

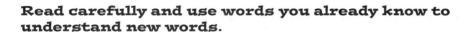

Read carefully and use words you already know to understand new words.

Directions: Read the passage below. Notice the context of the **boldface** words. Decide each boldface word's meaning and write your definitions on the lines.

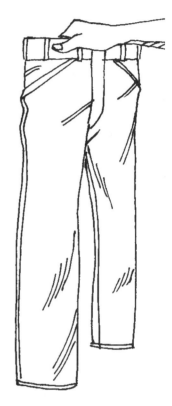

You've probably gone into a store and handed over money to **purchase** a product. If so, you have been a **consumer**. Usually, shoppers get what they pay for— but sometimes an item turns out to be a **dud**! That's when it's time to **complain**. When you get poor service or bad goods, don't waste time grumbling to friends. Go to those who can fix the problem. Explain what you need. Do you want a cash **refund** so you can buy a different product? Do you want to **exchange** the item for a similar one? Most **merchants** want to make customers happy. If you appear to be calm rather than **furious**, they will usually correct the problem.

1. To *purchase* must mean to _____.

2. I think that a *consumer* is _____.

3. I think *dud* means _____

   _____.

4. To *complain* must mean to _____

   _____.

5. I think that a *refund* is _____.

6. I think *exchange* means _____.

7. I think *merchants* are _____.

8. I think *furious* means _____.

Name: _____ **Date:** _____

It's time to do some original work. Just choose some words from the lessons to use in context.

A. **Directions:** Circle the word that best fits the context of the sentence.

1. The driver turned the car lights on at (twilight / throng).

2. The (consumer / merchant) sells video games and video tapes.

3. When the show is over, please leave by the nearest (exit / gully).

4. In the morning, I (arose / descended) from my sleep and got ready for school.

5. After you receive a gift, it is (dud / polite) to send a thank you note.

6. It took (panic / courage) to tell Mr. Burke that I broke his window.

7. Diving into (shallow / blind) water is very risky.

8. An unwrapped sandwich will quickly become (lively / stale).

B. **Directions:** Use each of the following words in a sentence. Make sure the context makes the word's meaning clear.

complain _____

_____

furious _____

_____

journey _____

_____

Name: _____   **Date:** _____

Every word either is a base word or contains one.
Sometimes other word parts are added to a base
word to make a new word.

EXAMPLE: free + dom = freedom

A. Directions: One word in each group is a base word. Circle it.

1. straight   straighter   straighten
2. open   openness   opener
3. renew   newly   new
4. taking   take   mistake
5. lowly   lower   low
6. home   homeward   homes
7. precook   cooks   cook
8. spelling   misspell   spell
9. zipper   zip   unzip
10. appear   disappear   appears

B. Directions: Each column begins with a base word. Circle two words in the list that have been formed from that word.

1. **long**
   longer
   longing
   lone

2. **pay**
   payment
   repay
   paper

3. **free**
   freeze
   freedom
   freely

4. **kind**
   kindly
   kin
   unkind

5. **hurt**
   hurtful
   hurting
   hurdle

6. **hum**
   hummed
   humming
   human

7. **do**
   dope
   doing
   redo

8. **smile**
   smiling
   mile
   smiles

Name: _____   Date: _____

Finding the base word in a longer word can help you figure out a new word's meaning.

A. Directions: Write the base word on each line.   **EXAMPLE:** helpless _____*help*_____

1. worker _____
2. surprising _____
3. useful _____
4. slightly _____
5. asked _____
6. nearest _____
7. remake _____
8. unhappy _____
9. hopeful _____
10. grasped _____
11. tied _____
12. searched _____

13. American _____
14. foolish _____
15. hunter _____
16. dances _____
17. easy _____
18. winner _____
19. sooner _____
20. nonfat _____
21. magical _____
22. forceful _____
23. wealthy _____
24. drifting _____

B. Directions: Complete each sentence with one of the base words you wrote above.

1. After the snowstorm, our car was buried in a _____.

2. "Abracadabra!" exclaimed Waldo the Wonderful as he performed his _____ act.

3. The pilgrims sailed the *Mayflower* to the country we now call _____.

Name: _____   Date: _____

Think about it. Can you name two or three words that have one base word in common?

Directions: Read the three words in each item. Then write the base word that the three words share. Finally, complete each sentence with one of the words.

EXAMPLE: refreshing   fresher   freshly   BASE WORD: _fresh_
a. Nothing smells better than _freshly_ baked bread!
b. Bread baked this morning will be _fresher_ than yesterday's bread.
c. After working on a hot day, I love a _refreshing_ swim in the pool.

1. **attracting   attractive   attraction**   BASE WORD: _____

   a. The roller coaster is the most thrilling _____ at the park.

   b. The sugar cookies are _____ ants to our picnic.

   c. Theo painted his house to make it more _____.

2. **invented   invention   inventor**   BASE WORD: _____

   a. Thomas Edison is remembered as a famous _____.

   b. He _____ the electric light bulb.

   c. Can you imagine what life would be like without Edison's
   _____?

3. **unthinkable   rethink   thinking**   BASE WORD: _____

   a. If the Johnsons can't find a babysitter, they'll have to
   _____ their evening's plans.

   b. Leaving a small child home alone is an _____ thing to do!

   c. Maggie Johnson is _____ about moving the party to
   her house.

4. **placed   placement   replace**   BASE WORD: _____

   a. If you break that antique vase, it will be hard to _____ it.

   b. Handle it gently and be careful with its _____ on the shelf.

   c. Watch out! I think you have _____ it too near the edge.

Name: _____   **Date:** _____

Are you ready for more practice with base words?

Directions: Read each sentence and the question that follows it. The base word of one of the words in the sentence will answer the question. Write that answer on the line.

EXAMPLE: *Over 2,000 years ago, the Chinese built the Great Wall.*

In what country would you find the Great Wall? ___*China*___

1. *Some people call a full moon a "lover's moon."*

   What emotion is said to be sparked by the full moon?

   _____

2. *Wolves are often heard howling at the full moon.*

   What do wolves sometimes do when the moon is full?

   _____

3. *In some places, farmers think it is good luck to plant crops under a new, or dark, moon.*

   What do we call a place in the country where crops are grown and animals are raised?

   _____

4. *Stories say "Don't look over your left shoulder during a new moon. It can bring misfortune!"*

   What is another word for "good luck"?

   _____

5. *Circling the Earth takes the moon about a month.*

   What is the word for a round disk shaped like a full moon?

   _____

Name: _____   **Date:** _____

A *prefix* is a group of letters added to the beginning of a base word. The result is a new word with its own meaning. For example: *un-* + *happy* = *unhappy*.

A. **Directions:** Write the prefix of each word on the line.

EXAMPLE: replace ___*re-*___

1. undo _____
2. preview _____
3. rebuild _____
4. disagree _____
5. bicycle _____

6. semicircle _____
7. foreground _____
8. supernatural _____
9. mislead _____
10. postwar _____

B. **Directions:** Add a prefix to the **boldface** word. Use the new word to complete the sentence.

EXAMPLE: **(turn)** If you don't like the gift, be sure to __*return*__ it.

1. **(appear)** The magician showed us a rabbit and then made it _____.

2. **(healthy)** The poor, stray dog looked thin and _____.

3. **(dress)** Before gym class, we have to _____ and put on our sweatsuits.

4. **(star)** The rock singer became so famous he was called a _____.

5. **(teen)** At age 12, Christina was a _____.

Name: _____   **Date:** _____

Every prefix has its own meaning. Understanding the prefix can help you figure out the meaning of the whole word.

A. Directions: The prefix *re-* means *again*. Read each sentence as it is. Then add the prefix *re-* to the beginning of the **boldface** word. As you read the sentence again, notice how the word's meaning has changed.

1. The directions told me to ____**read** the sentence.

2. I made a mistake and had to ____**do** the worksheet.

3. The office lost my paperwork, so I had to ____**apply** for the job.

B. Directions: The prefix *super-* means *above* or *more than normal*. Read each sentence as it is. Then add the prefix *super-* to the beginning of the **boldface** word. Read the sentence again and notice how the meaning has changed.

1. Marvelman is a _____**human** hero.

2. In today's world, the United States is a _____**power**.

3. Route 66 is a _____**highway** that crosses the nation.

C. Directions: The prefix *un-* means *not*. Read each sentence as it is. Then add the prefix *un-* to the beginning of the **boldface** word. Read the sentence again and notice how the meaning has changed.

1. Students like Ms. Chin because she never says ____**kind** things.

2. Some folks say that walking under open ladders is ____**lucky**.

3. Don't spend too much time worrying about ____**important** matters.

Name: _____ **Date:** _____

Here's some practice using those word starters known as *prefixes*.

Directions: Use the prefix *un-*, *re-*, or *super-* to write one word that replaces the **boldface** words.

EXAMPLE: I left the room with my test paper **not finished**. ___*unfinished*___

1. I heard a story about a flying dog, but I believe it was **not true**.

   _____

2. The photo came out so badly that I had to **take** it **over again**.

   _____

3. Is it a bird? Is it a plane? No! It's **the man who is greater than the average man**!

   _____

4. The sugar in the blue box is **finer than usual** sugar.   _____

5. It is **not safe** to ride a bike at night without a light.   _____

6. The gift arrived **without any wrapping on it**.   _____

7. The camera is out of focus, so you'll need to **adjust** the lens **again**.   _____

8. If the customer is not satisfied, the car wash will **wash** the car **again**.   _____

9. "Your paper is too short," said the teacher. "You'll need to **write** it **again**."   _____

10. The corner grocery won't have everything on your list, but the **large market that carries many more items** will.   _____

Name: _____   Date: _____

This exercise will show you what a *big* difference a prefix can make!

Directions: Read the following paragraph, and circle the words that have the prefix *un-*. Then rewrite the paragraph, removing the prefix *un-* wherever you find it.

Margo was unhappy with her school. The teachers, she felt, were quite unkind. The students were unfriendly. Margo got unsatisfactory grades, and she felt the grading system was unfair. The school staff treated Margo as if she were a very unimportant person. She felt like a most unlucky girl, indeed.

New Paragraph:

_____

_____

_____

_____

_____

_____

_____

_____

Name: _____   **Date:** _____

A *suffix* is a group of letters added to the end of a base word. Here's an example for you: *good* + *-ness* = *goodness*.

A. Directions: Write the *suffix* you see in each word.   **EXAMPLE:** peaceful ___*-ful*___

1. lonely _____   6. foolish _____

2. narrower _____   7. protection _____

3. hopeful _____   8. machinist _____

4. hopeless _____   9. building _____

5. government _____   10. builder _____

B. Directions: Add a suffix to the **boldface** word. Use the new word to complete the sentence.

EXAMPLE: **follow**

Sam didn't run for president because he's more of a ___*follower*___ than a leader.

1. **(honest)**   I _____ don't know who took Mr. Wilson's wallet!

2. **(piano)**   The _____ played beautiful music on the baby grand.

3. **(bake)**   The _____ made a special cake for the graduation party.

4. **(peace)**   When the violent storm ended, the valley was _____ again.

5. **(use)**   That camera will be _____ if there's no film in it.

Name: _____   **Date:** _____

Like a prefix, a suffix can completely change the meaning of a word.

Directions: The suffix *-less* means *without*. The suffix *-ful* means *full of*. You can create a pair of *antonyms* (opposites) by adding these suffixes to base words. Write sentences of your own using the antonyms below.

1. **fearless:** _____

   _____

   _____

   fearful: _____

   _____

   _____

2. **hopeless:** _____

   _____

   hopeful: _____

   _____

3. **colorless:** _____

   _____

   colorful: _____

   _____

4. **joyless:** _____

   _____

   joyful: _____

   _____

Name: _____ **Date:** _____

Who did it? To name people who "do" something, you can add the **suffix -er, -or, -eer, or -ist.**

Directions: Add a suffix to answer the question. Hint: The word you build will have the same base word as the **boldface** word.

EXAMPLE: Who **built** the new house on the corner? the _builder_

1. Who **acted** in the school play?　　　　　　　　the _____

2. Who painted the picture for the **art** show?　　the _____

3. Who **invented** that marvelous machine?　　　the _____

4. Who mixed the chemicals for the **scientific** study?　the _____

5. Who went down the **mine** shaft to dig out the ore?　the _____

6. Who **sings** the national anthem before the basketball game?　　　　　　　the _____

7. Who **teaches** students about prefixes and suffixes?

   the _____

8. Who moves the strings of the **puppets**?

   the _____

9. Who **conducts** the orchestra?

   the _____

10. Who drives the train **engine**?

    the _____

super　　ment ish
un　　　ful ion
re　post ist
pre　mis　er
des　　　ing
bi　　　less
semi　　ly
fore

Name: _____　　**Date:** _____

Unlock word meanings to show you have smarts.
Study words closely and notice their parts.

Directions: Use what you know about base words, suffixes, and prefixes to complete the crossword puzzle.

ACROSS

1. suffix meaning "full of"

3. prefix meaning "above" or "more than the usual"

7. a person who performs in a play

9. being without hope

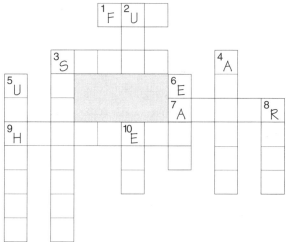

DOWN

2. base word shared by *useful* and *useless*

3. base word of *surprising*

4. one who creates works of art

5. not happy

6. base word of *easy*

8. to do over

10. suffix added to *puppet* to name the person who pulls the strings

Name: _____   **Date:** _____

A compound word joins two words as one. Usually, one plus one is two. In the case of a compound word, one plus one equals ONE! Example: side + walk = sidewalk

Directions: Circle the compound word in each sentence.

1. Some sports fans say that baseball is America's greatest sport.

2. On the school playground you can often see kids with bats and balls.

3. Students in Ms. Klein's classroom challenged Mr. Toro's students to a game.

4. My classmates decided that I should be catcher for Ms. Klein's team.

5. The morning of the big game, I looked everywhere for my old mitt.

6. How can a catcher catch without a mitt?

7. After a frantic search, I finally found the mitt upstairs.

8. It was lying forgotten in my bedroom closet.

9. By afternoon, the two excited teams were on the field.

10. "Oh, no," I groaned as raindrops fell.

11. We went inside to wait out the storm.

Name: _____   **Date:** _____

Inside, outside, here and there . . . You'll find compound words most everywhere! If you can find three compound words in that rhyme, you're ready for this activity.

A. Directions: Combine a word from the first column with a word from the second column to make a compound word. Write the compound words on the lines.

COLUMN 1	COLUMN 2
rain	thing
home	bow
touch	sick
snow	down
any	mobile

COMPOUND WORDS

_____

_____

_____

_____

_____

B. Directions: Now complete each sentence with one of the compound words you wrote above.

1. After the storm, the sun came out, and a colorful _____ arched over our heads.

2. The quarterback threw a pass and the receiver made a _____.

3. Nick was lonely and _____ during his first days at summer camp.

4. The _____ zoomed across the winter meadow.

5. We'll meet at six, but if _____ changes, call me!

Name: _____   **Date:** _____

Once again, it's time to use your vocabulary skills and poetic talents!

Directions: Combine words listed below to make a compound word that completes each rhyme. Hint: You'll use one word twice.

ball
day
break
fire
foot
hall
prints
sun
set
way
wood

1. When the leaves drop in the fall

   Autumn sports fans watch _____.

2. I'd start a fire if I could,

   But the rain soaked all our _____.

3. The sky was red when the pair first met

   Sitting on a beach watching the _____.

4. Come on inside! I hope you'll stay.

   Just hang your coat in the _____.

5. It's six o'clock, and I'm awake!

   I'm up and ready at _____.

6. The mystery's solved. Among the hints

   Was a set of the suspect's _____.

Remember that a *compound word* combines two
or more words to make a new word.

A. **Directions:** Write a compound word on the line to answer each question.

1. In what do sparrows and
   robins clean themselves?

   _____

2. What time of day follows noon
   and comes before evening?

   _____

3. What does an artist use to
   apply color to a canvas?

   _____

4. What is a popular American sport? _____

B. **Directions:** Now use each of the compound words you wrote above in a sentence.

1. _____
   _____

2. _____
   _____

3. _____
   _____

4. _____
   _____

Name: _____   **Date:** _____

Notice the apostrophe between the *t* and the *s* in *what's*? You'll always find an apostrophe in a contraction.

A. **Directions:** A contraction is a shortened word made from two or more words. An apostrophe (') shows where one or more letters have been left out.

      EXAMPLE: what + is = what's

Write the two words that are joined in each contraction below.
The first one has been done for you.

1. isn't = *is not*

2. wouldn't = _____

3. you'll = _____

4. she's = _____

5. didn't = _____

6. I've = _____

7. there's = _____

8. we're = _____

9. I'm = _____

10. let's = _____

B. **Directions:** Now write the contraction of each set of words below.

1. could not = *couldn't*

2. you have = _____

3. here is = _____

4. he would = _____

5. who is = _____

6. I had = _____

7. that is = _____

8. would not = _____

9. where is = _____

10. were not = _____

Get ready for some more contraction action!

A. Directions: Replace the **boldface** words with a contraction. Write the contraction on the line.

1. You **should not** throw that banana peel away! _____

2. **There is** more than one thing you can do with it. _____

3. If you turn it upside down, **it will** make an excellent hat for a tiny head. _____

4. Amy says **she will** watch her banana peel turn brown. _____

5. I hope you **did not** leave your peel on the ground! _____

6. If you had, someone **might have** slipped on it! _____

B. Directions: Circle the contraction in each sentence. Rewrite the sentence replacing the contraction with the two words that it combines.

1. What's the matter? _____

2. Don't you feel well? _____

3. Maybe you've caught a cold. _____

4. You'll likely feel better soon. _____

5. I'm sure of it! _____

6. You shouldn't go to the party with a cold. _____

_____

Name: _____ **Date:** _____

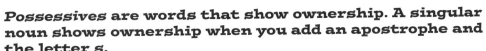

Possessives are words that show ownership. A singular noun shows ownership when you add an apostrophe and the letter *s*.

A. **Directions:** Circle the possessive form that correctly completes each sentence. Then write the word in the blank.

1. A _____ nose is amazing.

   hounds / hound's / hound,s

2. A hound can smell a small _____ trail long before it can see the creature.

   animal's / animals / amina'ls

3. A _____ long ears and sharp nose make it a typical hound.

   beagle / beagl'es / beagle's

4. In the wilderness, the hound is a _____ friend and partner.

   hunters' / hunter's / hunters

5. Unlike most hounds, a _____ sight is its sharpest sense.

   greyhounds / greyhound's / greyhound

6. Because it can sniff out a criminal or lost person, a bloodhound is the _____ greatest detective dog.

   world's / world / worlds'

B. **Directions:** Complete each sentence with a noun that shows ownership.

1. The _____ leash is hanging on the hook.

2. The _____ feathers are on the floor of the cage.

3. The _____ horn would not stop honking.

4. Did you see that _____ strange hairdo?

Name: _____ **Date:** _____

> Most plural nouns end in *s*. To make them possessive, put the apostrophe at the end of the word.

A. **Directions:** After each sentence, write the noun that shows ownership and the object owned. Use the possessive form.

EXAMPLE: The hats of the ladies are silly.

ladies' hats

1. The teams of both schools are winners. _____

2. The routines of the clowns were funny. _____

3. The ringing of the bells announced the time. _____

4. These robes belong to the choir members. _____

5. The hum of mosquitoes reminded me that
   it was summer. _____

B. **Directions:** Some plural nouns end in a letter other than *s*. To make them possessive, add an apostrophe plus *s*. Complete each sentence. Write the possessive form of a word from the box.

children
mice
oxen
geese

1. The _____ toys filled the playroom.

2. The wagon trail was marked by the _____ hoofprints.

3. We could hear the _____ tiny sounds in the attic.

4. Each fall, the _____ flight path takes them over our city.

Name: _____   **Date:** _____

 Building Vocabulary Skills and Strategies, Level 3 • Saddleback Publishing, Inc. ©2004 • 3 Watson, Irvine, CA 92618 • Phone (888) SDL-BACK • www.sdlback.com

Practice what you've learned about compound words and words with apostrophes.

A. **Directions:** Combine two words listed below to make compound words. Try different combinations, and create as many compound words as you can!

sea	home	sick	shore	line	plane	air	side	out

_____   _____   _____

_____   _____   _____

_____   _____   _____

B. **Directions:** Write each word from the box under the correct heading. Then use one word from each column in a sentence.

couldn't	cannot	he's	men's	Julia's	what's	inside

COMPOUND WORDS: CONTRACTIONS: POSSESSIVES:

_____   _____   _____

_____   _____   _____

_____   _____   _____

MY SENTENCES:

1. _____

2. _____

3. _____

Stretch your mind with this vocabulary exercise.

Directions: Write a word that matches the first definition. Then double one letter to spell a word that matches the second definition.

EXAMPLE: Slang word for a police officer = _____cop_____

A place where chickens are kept = _____coop_____

1. Very, very warm = _____

   An owl's call = _____

2. Your male baby = _____

   Before long = _____

3. To make a wager = _____

   A dark red vegetable = _____

4. Messy food fed to pigs = _____

   A type of boat = _____

5. The number following nine = _____

   Someone age 13 to 19 = _____

6. A written sales pitch = _____

   To put two and two together = _____

7. To place something somewhere = _____

   To make a golf shot on the green = _____

8. Longing for something to happen = _____

   Jumping up and down on one foot = _____

Name: _____   Date: _____

Did you mean *night* or *knight*? You probably can't tell by the sound of the word. *Night* and *knight* are *homonyms*—different words that sound alike.

A. Directions: Notice the homonyms in parentheses as you read each sentence. Circle the correct homonym.

1. If you (need / knead) something to spice up a meal, you might try ketchup.

2. Ketchup is a sauce (made / maid) from tomatoes, sugar, salt, mustard, vinegar, and spices.

3. The name (four / for) the sauce is believed to have come from an Asian word pronounced "kaychup."

4. The word we use is not only spelled "ketchup," but "catchup" or "catsup," (two / too).

5. You can (buy / by) ketchup in almost any grocery store.

6. The tangy, red sauce tastes (great / grate) on (stake / steak).

B. Directions: Unscramble the letters to spell the homonym of the **boldface** word. Then write sentences using the words you unscrambled.

1. **been**   N I B   _____

2. **hair**   R H E A   _____

3. **pair**   R E A P   _____

4. **dough**   E D O   _____

_____

_____

_____

_____

See and *sea* are different words that sound alike.
That makes them homonyms.

Directions: Fill in each blank with the correct homonym.

1. **whole / hole**

   a. I can't believe I ate the _____ box of donuts!

   b. To be a donut, a round cake must have a _____.

2. **principal / principle**

   a. Honesty is a _____ to live by!

   b. Ms. Chin, our school _____, announced the guest speaker.

3. **flee / flea**

   a. Waldo found a _____ in his dog's thick coat.

   b. If the fire comes their way, the animals must _____ the forest.

4. **plain / plane**

   a. Would you like a _____ or chocolate donut?

   b. The wings dipped as the _____ turned.

5. **sleigh/ slay**

   a. The horse pulled the _____ through the snowy field.

   b. The young hero will _____ the fierce dragon.

6. **rain / reign**

   a. The homecoming queen will _____ at the football game.

   b. I hope it doesn't _____ during the game.

7. **throne / thrown**

   a. The ball was _____ from the 20-yard line.

   b. The queen sat on a _____ decorated with flowers.

Name: _____ **Date:** _____

Do you eat *dessert or desert?* Choose the second word and you'll get a mouthful of sand! These two words are among the many that people often confuse.

Directions: Circle the word that correctly completes each sentence. Use a dictionary if you need help deciding which word is correct.

1. Cactus is the name of a family of plants that often grow in the (dessert / desert).

2. A cactus is able to live in very dry (weather / whether).

3. Most plants (lose / loose) water through their leaves.

4. The cactus has very few leaves, and it stores water in (it's / its) stem.

5. The plant can live (quiet / quit / quite) a long time without water.

6. The (whole / hole) cactus plant is covered with bristles and spines.

7. If an animal bites into those spines, it will quickly (quiet / quit / quite) eating!

8. All cactus plants, (except / accept) a few, sprout beautiful flowers.

9. Even a cactus will (dye / die) without water.

10. Cactus roots are (clothes / close) to the surface so they can catch any water that falls.

CHALLENGE: Do you know the *plural* form of cactus?

Check a dictionary and write it here: _____

Name: _____

Date: _____

This lesson will set you
straight on some words that
many people find confusing.

Directions: Fill in the blanks with the words that
correctly complete the sentences.
Use a dictionary if you need help.

1. **presents / presence**

   a. The royal subjects bowed in
   the _____ of the king.

   b. The greedy king demanded that
   people bring him money and
   _____.

2. **chose / choose**

   a. Of all the people in our school, Michael _____
   Ricky for his best friend.

   b. Who did you _____ to be among your group of friends?

3. **led / lead**

   a. I think the new president will _____ the country well.

   b. When he was governor, he _____ his state to better times.

4. **advice / advise**

   a. Take my _____ and get to the stadium early.

   b. I _____ you to buy game tickets online at a low price.

5. **past / passed**

   a. What happened yesterday is in the _____.

   b. I'm sorry that I _____ up a chance to learn to ski.

6. **lose / loose**

   a. It looked like our team would _____ the game.

   b. I untied the leash and let the dog _____.

Name: _____   **Date:** _____

Help! This ad writer mixed up some homonyms and easily confused words! Can you fix the mistakes?

Directions: The **boldface** words in the following advertisement are incorrect! Write the correct word next to the matching number.

Do you **knead** (1) a better bread?

Smart shoppers will **chose** (2)

Crackle Top

Crackle Top is **maid** (3) fresh

daily from **hole** (4) grains.

At a low, low price, it is a wise **by** (5).

For a **grate** (6) sandwich, try Crackle Top with leftover **stake** (7).

Sprinkle sugar on toasted Crackle Top for a sweet **desert** (8).

• •

Ask for Crackle Top at your **supper** (9) market!

Don't **except** (10) a substitute.

1. _____   6. _____

2. _____   7. _____

3. _____   8. _____

4. _____   9. _____

5. _____   10. _____

Name: _____   **Date:** _____

Your vocabulary skills come into play in the game of "Take-Away."

Directions: Write a word that matches the first definition. Then take away one letter to write a word that matches the second definition.

1. a. a stick carried to
        help with walking: _____

    b. a round, metal container
        in which foods are sealed: _____

2. a. a group of musicians playing together: _____

    b. the opposite of good: _____

3. a. a growing, living thing that
        usually has a stem and leaves: _____

    b. a thought-out way of doing something: _____

4. a. a measure of the moment, such as one o'clock: _____

    b. to bind together with string: _____

5. a. a soft, furry animal with long ears and a short tail: _____

    b. a Jewish leader: _____

6. a. the past tense of *steal*: _____

    b. the bottom surface of your foot: _____

7. a. a pipe for carrying away water: _____

    b. water drops that fall from the sky: _____

8. a. to make a picture with a pencil or pen: _____

    b. uncooked: _____

9. a. a measure of volume that equals $1/2$ quart: _____

    b. a stiff wire with one flat end and one
        pointed end that fastens things together: _____

Name: _____   Date: _____

Give your vocabulary skills some exercise. Add a rhyming word to complete each verse.

Directions: Complete each rhyme. Write a word from the box on the line. The word you write should match the definition in parentheses.

agile	awl	bouquet	cousin	drought	grumpy	plummet

1. Wanda was first in the game of croquet.

   She won a beautiful tulip _____.
   (bunch of flowers)

2. The rain comes down! "Hurrah!" we shout.

   This puts an end to the month-long _____.
   (dry spell)

3. "Come help me work!" I heard the call.

   The cobbler said, "Hand me the _____."
   (pointed tool used to punch holes)

4. Aunt Sal baked pies, about a dozen.

   She made them for me and my _____.
   (the child of your aunt or uncle)

5. I'm looking down from the mountain's summit.

   If I slipped, I'd have a long way to _____.
   (fall straight down)

6. "Don't trip now, Ben! That vase is fragile!"

   Ben's mother knows her son isn't _____.
   (able to move easily)

7. The sheets were cold; the bed was lumpy.

   I've had no sleep, and I am _____.
   (in a bad mood)

Name: _____   **Date:** _____

Do you say *taxicab*, *cab*, or *taxi*? Many words have shortened forms that are more commonly used.

A. Directions: Write the shortened form of each of the following words.

EXAMPLE: professional = _pro_

1. photograph = _____

2. mathematics = _____

3. advertisement = _____

4. popular = _____

5. telephone = _____

6. gasoline = _____

7. microphone = _____

8. airplane = _____

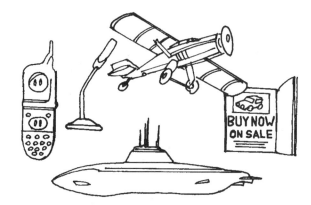

9. professor = _____

10. submarine or substitute = _____

B. Directions: Read the following story. Circle words that are shortened forms of longer words. (You should circle seven words.)

The Winner

The school assembly began. My English prof was going to announce the winner of the writing contest. He stepped up to the mike. I waited anxiously. The contest prize was a plane trip to Hollywood and a ticket to a pop music concert! Now, I may not be very good at science or math, but I'm a real pro at English! This was my big day! My pal Veronica snapped a photo of me happily accepting my prize.

Name: _____   **Date:** _____

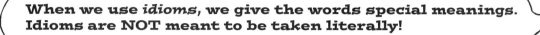

When we use *idioms*, we give the words special meanings. Idioms are NOT meant to be taken literally!

EXAMPLE: My English teacher is a *rare bird!*

EXPLANATION: The teacher is not *really* a bird, of course. This idiom means that the teacher has some very unusual qualities.

Directions: Read each pair of sentences. Circle the letter of the sentence that contains an idiom.

Miss Peacock

1. a. When I waded into the ocean, I got cold feet.

   b. I was supposed to give a speech, but I got cold feet.

2. a. Summer is our rainy season, and when it rains, it pours.

   b. After getting a flat tire and losing my wallet, I realized that when it rains, it pours.

3. a. Hoping to break the ice, Owen told the new girl a joke.

   b. When you go ice fishing, use this hatchet to break the ice.

4. a. I aimed, pulled the bow string, and the arrow hit the spot.

   b. On a hot day, a cold glass of lemonade really hits the spot.

5. a. When Bill left the farm and moved to the city, he felt like a fish out of water.

   b. A fish out of water only stays fresh for a few days.

 Name: _____   **Date:** _____

An idiom can be a colorful way of expressing an idea.

Directions: Replace the **boldface** words in each sentence with one of the idioms in the box.

Don't cry over spilled milk.   in hot water
Two heads are better than one.   turn over a new leaf
getting a taste of your own medicine

1. Will you help me with my homework? **I know that we can do better if we work together**.

   _____

2. Don't break the school rules. If you do, you might find yourself **in big trouble**.

   _____

3. You laughed at Sally when she slipped and fell. Now people are laughing at you for dropping your books. It looks like you're **getting back just what you gave**.

   _____

4. It's too bad you broke your grandmother's china plate. Now it's time to get over it. **Don't spend time worrying about a past event**.

   _____

5. I haven't been studying enough. I want better grades, so I'm going to **change my ways** and spend more time on my homework!

   _____

Name: _____   **Date:** _____

> Some words create clearer pictures than others. Whenever you can, pep up your writing by using *vivid* words.

A. Directions: Circle the word in each group that creates the clearest picture.

1. walked   waddled   moved

2. spoke   talked   babbled

3. building   skyscraper   structure

4. house   home   mansion

5. toddler   kid   child

6. dish   plate   china

B. Directions: Write a sentence using each word you circled above.

1. _____

2. _____

3. _____

4. _____

5. _____

6. _____

Name: _____   **Date:** _____

VIVID WORDS THAT MAKE A SOUND

Some words imitate sounds. They help us *hear* the meaning.

A. Directions: Read the paragraph. Circle the words that create a sound.

Things were going wrong with our car. A loud clank came from the rear. Sometimes the engine purred smoothly, but sometimes it squealed like a pig. The radio no longer played music. Instead, it put out a steady buzz. The pitter-patter of rain against the windows made me nervous. The windshield wipers seldom worked. Instead of going swish in a steady rhythm, they went creak, clink, screech. I think the time has come for us to get a new car.

B. Directions: On the line below, write sentences using the following "noisy" words:

boom   honk   rattle   thump

1. _____

_____

2. _____

_____

3. _____

_____

4. _____

_____

Name: _____   Date: _____

> Some words are too general to be very descriptive. Other words are more specific—they narrow the meaning. For example, the word *summer* is more specific than the word *season*. It limits the idea and creates a clearer meaning.

A. **Directions:** Circle the most specific word in each pair below.

1. The Dorfmunder family has a new (dog / spaniel).

2. Most (teens / people) like loud music.

3. My family likes to go out for (meal / breakfast) on Saturday mornings.

4. Traffic slowed to a crawl because of the (bad / icy) weather.

5. Marcus felt nervous as he entered the (building / hospital).

6. "Hurrah! I won!" (exclaimed / said) the golfer.

7. People liked Marjorie Lee because she was (nice / generous).

8. I often eat spinach because it is quite (tasty / good).

B. **Directions:** Write a more specific word for each general word below.

　　　　　　EXAMPLE: vehicle / *bus*

1. house / _____
2. bird / _____
3. said / _____
4. dessert / _____

5. fish / _____
6. vegetable / _____
7. bad / _____
8. street / _____

Name: _____　　**Date:** _____

Present a clear idea by using words that are specific rather than general.

EXAMPLE:

We cancelled the picnic because of the **weather**.
(GENERAL)

We cancelled the picnic because of the **rainstorm** (or **heat**).
(SPECIFIC)   (SPECIFIC)

Directions: Rewrite each sentence to make the meaning clearer. Replace the **boldface** words with more specific words.

1. Kira's hair looks **nice** today.

   _____

2. Bowser is a **nice** dog.

   _____

3. My friend Ramon is **big**.

   _____

4. I saw a **bad** movie last night.

   _____

5. Did you see Chester's **clothes**?

   _____

6. The **room** was decorated for the party.

   _____

Name: _____   **Date:** _____

> Now it's time to review some of the "vivid" words you've been learning.

Directions: Unscramble the **boldface** letters to write one of the vivid vocabulary words from the previous four lessons.

1. the way a duck walks

   d l d e w a _____

2. the noise a bee makes

   z u z b _____

3. a small child who has just learned to walk

   d l o t r e d _____

4. to say something with excitement

   x l m a i c e _____

5. a large, expensive house

   s a m n i n o _____

6. the noise a cannon makes

   m o b o _____

7. the sound of a horn

   n h k o _____

8. a very tall building

   k e y p a s s c r r _____

Name: _____   **Date:** _____

Some words can be more than one part of speech. A word's part of speech depends on the way it is used in a sentence.

Directions: Read each sentence. Decide if the **boldface** word is a *noun* (names a person, place, or thing), *verb* (expresses action), or *adjective* (describes). Write the part of speech on the line.

1. a. The golf ball bounced onto the **green**. _____

   b. The **green** tree frog blended with the leaves. _____

2. a. Begin the job by making a step-by-step **plan**. _____

   b. Christina will **plan** the project, but I will do the work. _____

3. a. **Grease** the wheels to make them turn silently. _____

   b. The mechanic had **grease** on his uniform. _____

4. a. The wheat was **ground** into flour. _____

   b. The **ground** is too wet for a picnic. _____

5. a. My little brother is afraid of the **dark**. _____

   b. We couldn't find our seats in the **dark** theater. _____

6. a. The **play** was divided into three acts. _____

   b. Don't **play** your drums when the neighbors are sleeping. _____

7. a. If you want to grow vegetables, you must **weed** the garden. _____

   b. The dandelion is a common **weed**. _____

8. a. The **search** took the men deep into the forest. _____

   b. I'm going to **search** for my lost wallet. _____

Name: _____   **Date:** _____

Figure out whether the vocabulary words on this page are used as *nouns* or *verbs*. Read the sentences carefully!

Directions: Fill in the blank with one of the words from the box. In the brackets after the sentence, write *noun* or *verb* to tell the word's part of speech. The first one has been done for you as an example.

blanket	dance	drive	joke	reward

1. The tango is a romantic Latin __*dance*__. [_*noun*_]

2. Do you like to _____ the tango? [_____]

3. If you're leaving now, Jason can _____ you home. [_____]

4. The _____ on the curvy road made Celia carsick. [_____]

5. When my dog Skipper sits, I _____ him with a biscuit. [_____]

6. Jessie offered a $50 _____ for the return of her ring. [_____]

7. A wool _____ is warmer than a cotton one. [_____]

8. The snow will _____ the city streets by morning. [_____]

9. Dr. Klein will _____ with his patients to make them laugh. [_____]

10. Have you heard the funny _____ about the alligator and the duck? [_____]

Name: _____   **Date:** _____

Is the word a *verb*, a *noun*, or an *adjective*? Does it show an action, name something, or describe something?

Directions: Read the following paragraph. On the lines after the paragraph, write the parts of speech of the numbered words.

HELPING HANDS

Most people know that Seeing Eye dogs can <u>help</u> blind people in their daily

(1)
lives. Did you know that monkeys can be a <u>help</u> to disabled people, too? A

(2)
group that <u>calls</u> itself "Helping Hands"

(3)
<u>trains</u> monkeys to do chores such as

(4)
turn on lights and retrieve objects. The monkeys can even pick up the phone to answer incoming <u>calls</u>!

(5)

While animals don't usually ride on <u>public</u> transportation, animal helpers

(6)
can board buses and <u>trains</u> with their

(7)
owners. Donations from the <u>public</u> pay

(8)
for the Helping Hands program.

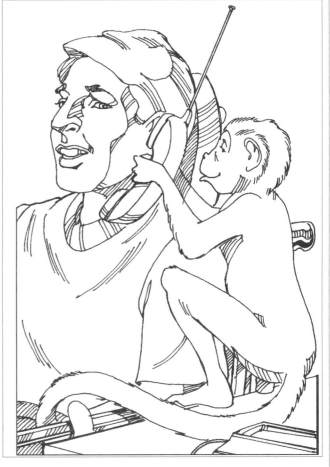

1. _____   5. _____

2. _____   6. _____

3. _____   7. _____

4. _____   8. _____

Name: _____   **Date:** _____

To fully understand a word, think about all the different ways it might be used.

Directions: Write original sentences using the **boldface** words as the parts of speech indicated.

1. **coat**

   NOUN: _____

   _____

   VERB: _____

   _____

2. **paste**

   NOUN: _____

   _____

   VERB: _____

   _____

3. **brush**

   NOUN: _____

   VERB: _____

4. **head**

   NOUN: _____

   VERB: _____

5. **deep**

   NOUN: _____

   VERB: _____

6. **clean**

   NOUN: _____

   VERB: _____

Name: _____   **Date:** _____

Check your understanding of the words you use. It helps to think about their parts of speech.

Directions: Circle the part of speech of the **boldface** word.

1. Angela made a careful **plan** before planting her garden.

   noun   verb   adjective

2. She wanted plants that would **help** attract butterflies.

   noun   verb   adjective

3. Butterflies like warmth, so Angela planted on the sunny, **back** side of the house.

   noun   verb   adjective

4. She knew she would have to **weed** the garden each week.

   noun   verb   adjective

5. She left the thistles because butterflies are drawn to that **weed**.

   noun   verb   adjective

6. Angela has a **green** thumb, so her garden grew healthy and bright.

   noun   verb   adjective

7. She planted colorful flowers and waited for butterflies to **dance** from blossom to blossom.

   noun   verb   adjective

8. When the job of caring for the garden became too much, Angela hired some **help**.

   noun   verb   adjective

9. Angela's hard work brought her a wonderful **reward**.

   noun   verb   adjective

10. She can **plan** on watching butterflies each summer day.

   noun   verb   adjective

Name: _____

Date: _____

Adverbs **add meaning to verbs, adjectives, and other adverbs. They usually end in the letters** *-ly.*

EXAMPLE: The jet-boat roared *swiftly* up the river.
It was an *extremely* powerful boat.

Directions: Choose the correct meaning of the **boldface** adverb. Circle the letter.

1. He plays the piano **splendidly**.
   a. like a beginner
   b. very well
   c. loudly

2. The cat was **obviously** hungry.
   a. clearly   b. very   c. not

3. Gina walked **gingerly** over the rocks.
   a. quickly   b. happily   c. carefully

4. Sometimes Tom drives **recklessly**.
   a. with great care
   b. without the proper care
   c. very slowly

5. Please finish the job **completely**.
   a. entirely   b. correctly   c. today

6. The plane landed **safely**.
   a. unharmed
   b. on time
   c. with damage

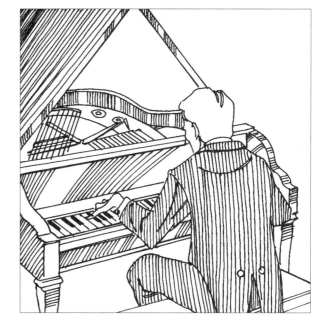

7. Maggie sobbed **mournfully**.
   a. with joy
   b. with great sorrow
   c. out loud

8. The building was **eerily** dark and quiet.
   a. very
   b. not very
   c. strangely

Name: _____   **Date:** _____

Show what you know about *adverbs*. Remember that these *-ly* words add meaning to verbs.

A. Directions: Rewrite an adjective from the word box as an adverb. Write it on the line to complete the sentence.

angry	comfortable	joyful	perfect	rich	tearful

1. We cheered _____ when our team won the trophy.

2. It's impossible to sit _____ on the hard, wooden bench.

3. The ring was _____ decorated with many diamonds and pearls.

4. Nina sobbed _____ over the injured bird.

5. "Never do that again!" Hailey shouted _____.

6. "One hundred percent!" Justin exclaimed. "I answered the questions _____!"

B. Directions: Write three sentences of your own. Use three of the adverbs you wrote above.

1. _____

_____

2. _____

_____

3. _____

_____

Name: _____ **Date:** _____

Build your vocabulary muscles with this word workout!

Directions: Use letters you find in the word VOCABULARY to write words that match each definition. See number 1 as an example.

1. the place in a truck where the driver sits *or* a car for hire

   <u>c</u> <u>a</u> <u>b</u>

2. to steal something

   — — —

3. the place a scientist works (short form)

   — — —

4. a curved body of water that cuts into the shoreline *or* to howl with long, deep sounds

   — — —

5. a narrow beam of light

   — — —

6. a lumpy, black substance used as fuel

   — — — —

7. having to do with a king or queen

   — — — — —

8. the hard, center part of an ear of corn

   — — —

9. having to do with the voice *or* speaking loudly and openly

   — — — — —

10. to be different *or* of great variety

   — — — —

Name: _____

Date: _____

Don't be afraid to work out with this assortment of absolutely amazing "A" words!

Directions: Think about each situation described below. Then write a couple of sentences describing the action. Use at least one of the "A" words in the box in each answer.

appreciate	anxious	annoyed	afraid	able	allow	amazing	awful

1. Sam and Sheila have missed the last bus home from the shopping mall. What might Sheila say to Sam?

_____

_____

_____

_____

_____

_____

_____

2. Gina is ending her job interview. What might she say to the employer?

_____

_____

_____

_____

_____

_____

3. The airplane is flying through a storm. What might the pilot announce to the passengers?

_____

_____

_____

_____

_____

_____

Name: _____

Date: _____

You know that dictionaries list words in alphabetical order. When looking up a word, you'll need to call on your alphabetizing know-how.

A. Directions: Which word would a dictionary list *first?* Circle the correct word in each pair.

1. hungry / happiness

2. suggest / support

3. bowl / bold

4. ballot/ ballet

5. eagle / doll

6. busy / business

7. habit / flea

8. parachute / practice

B. Directions: Rewrite the words below in alphabetical order.

RANDOM LIST	ALPHABETIZED LIST
globe	_____
famous	_____
reason	_____
thin	_____
answer	_____
forward	_____
vacation	_____
key	_____
breakfast	_____
apple	_____
brain	_____
ample	_____
foreign	_____
thick	_____
religion	_____

Name: _____

Date: _____

You'll find two guide words at the top of each dictionary page. One names the *first* entry word listed on that page. The other names the *last*. All entry words on that page fall alphabetically between the two guide words.

A. Directions: Look at the **boldface** guide words at the top of each dictionary page below. Then circle the words that would be defined on that page.

1.
noodle	**North Pole**

nor   nope   none

normal   nurse

3.
speedboat	**spice**

spell   speech   spend

spear   spill

2.
queen	**quick**

quarter   quicksand   quest

question   quilt

4.
zing	**zoom**

zip   zebra   zero

zoo   zone

B. Directions: Write one more word that would be found on a page headed with the guide words above. Hint: Name the picture below and you'll have one of the answers you need. If you need help with the others, use a dictionary.

1.
noodle	**North Pole**

2.
queen	**quick**

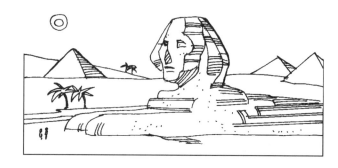

3.
speedboat	**spice**

4.
zing	**zoom**

Name: _____

Date: _____

Guide words name the first and last entry words found on a dictionary page. Here is some guide word practice.

A. Directions: Each box contains a set of guide words and their dictionary page number. On which page would each of the following words appear?

direct   disappear
p. 123

drive   drop
p. 130

drum   dude
p. 135

1. _____ dryer

2. _____ dirt

3. _____ droopy

4. _____ disable

5. _____ duct

6. _____ duchess

7. _____ drool

8. _____ disagree

9. _____ drizzle

10. _____ duck

B. Directions: Use your own dictionary to look up five of the words listed above. Write a definition for each word. (The guide words in your dictionary will probably be different from the ones that appear above.)

WORD

SENTENCE

1. _____ _____

2. _____ _____

3. _____ _____

4. _____ _____

5. _____ _____

Name: _____   **Date:** _____

Each sep·a·rate sound with·in a word is called a syl·la·ble. Rec·og·niz·ing syl·la·bles can help you spell words and say them cor·rect·ly. A dic·tion·ary shows you how to di·vide a word in·to its syl·la·bles. (Did you notice that the words you just read were divided into syllables?)

Directions: Circle the word in each group that is correctly divided into syllables. Use a dictionary for help.

1. **athlete**

   at•hle•te

   ath•lete

   a•th•lete

2. **soccer**

   soc•cer

   socc•er

   so•ccer

12. **exercise**

    exe•r•cise

    ex•erc•ise

    ex•er•cise

13. **hockey**

    hockey

    hock•ey

    hoc•key

3. **gymnasium**

   gy•mna•sium

   gym•na•si•um

   gym•na•sium

4. **stadium**

   sta•di•um

   st•ad•i•um

   stad•ium

5. **court**

   co•urt

   cou•rt

   court

6. **arena**

   a•re•na

   arena

   ar•e•na

7. **Olympics**

   Olymp•ics

   Oly•mp•ics

   O•lym•pics

8. **trophy**

   tro•phy

   troph•y

   tr•oph•y

9. **track**

   tr•ack

   track

   tra•ck

10. **tournament**

    tour•na•ment

    tou•rna•ment

    tour•nam•ent

11. **champion**

    cham•pi•on

    champ•ion

    champ•i•on

14. **race**

    race

    ra•ce

    r•ace

15. **relay**

    relay

    re•lay

    rel•ay

16. **victory**

    vic•tor•y

    vic•to•ry

    vict•o•ry

Name: _____ Date: _____

A. Directions: Circle only the one-syllable words in the box below.

view	route	lodging	trip
foreign	travel	train	hiker
confirm	inn	arrive	gate
rental	fare	price	map
	flight	guide	

B. Directions: Divide each word into syllables. Use a dictionary to check your work.

1. vacation

_____

2. reservation

_____

3. tourist

_____

4. summer

_____

5. departure

_____

6. ticket

_____

7. farewell

_____

8. recreation

_____

9. hotel

_____

10. airport

_____

11. destination

_____

12. backpack

_____

13. journey

_____

14. souvenir

_____

Name: _____   **Date:** _____

The dictionary can help you say words correctly. You'll find a respelling after the entry word. In words of two or more syllables, you'll see an accent mark (´). It shows you which syllable is emphasized, or said the hardest.

A. Directions: Circle the letter of the word that has the accent mark on the correct syllable. For help, say the word aloud. Use a dictionary to check your work.

1. **obey**
   a. o´ bey
   b. o bey´

2. **better**
   a. bet´ ter
   b. bet ter´

3. **remember**
   a. re´ mem ber
   b. re mem´ ber

4. **umbrella**
   a. um brel la´
   b. um brel´ la

5. **practice**
   a. prac´ tice
   b. prac tice´

6. **coyote**
   a. coy o´ te
   b. coy ot e´

B. Directions: Look up each word in the dictionary. Divide it into syllables. Then place an accent mark over the syllable that is emphasized. Use #1 as an example.

1. respect ____re spect´____

2. glory _____

3. metal _____

4. condemn _____

5. geyser _____

6. extra _____

7. meteor _____

8. rainstorm _____

9. declare _____

10. unclean _____

11. reply _____

12. muzzle _____

Name: _____   Date: _____

Some words have more than one meaning. In the dictionary, the different meanings will be numbered.

Directions: You'll find dictionary definitions in a box over each set of sentences. Write the number of the definition that matches the word's use in each sentence. Use the first item as an example.

---

companion **1:** a person who goes along with or spends time with another **2:** either one of a pair of matched things

1. __/__ Ms. Ramon is lonely and needs a **companion**.

2. __2__ Where is the **companion** to this sock?

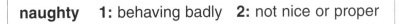

really **1:** in fact, actually **2:** very, to an extreme

3. _____ It was a **really** hot day.

4. _____ Is that **really** you under the mask?

naughty **1:** behaving badly **2:** not nice or proper

5. _____ No one would baby-sit for Owen Baker because he was so **naughty**.

6. _____ Owen used **naughty** words and threw toys around the room.

disturb **1:** to break up the peace and quiet **2:** to make worried or upset
3: to put into disorder

7. _____ The idea of a pop quiz **disturbs** me.

8. _____ The roar of the snowmobile **disturbed** the silent meadow.

9. _____ The child cried when someone **disturbed** his sandcastle.

Name: _____   **Date:** _____

When you come across a new word, you can find its meaning in a dictionary.

Directions: Look up each **boldface** word in a dictionary. Circle the letter of the correct definition, or meaning. Then use the word in a sentence.

1. **coward**
   a. a person who lacks courage
   b. a person who lacks wealth
   c. a person who is braver than most

   SENTENCE: _____
   _____
   _____
   _____

4. **shiny**
   a. bright and highly polished
   b. cheaply made
   c. very thin

   SENTENCE: _____
   _____
   _____
   _____

2. **illuminate**
   a. to heat up
   b. to become ill
   c. to light up

   SENTENCE: _____
   _____
   _____
   _____

3. **minstrel**
   a. a religious leader
   b. a coal miner
   c. a traveling singer

   SENTENCE: _____
   _____
   _____
   _____

5. **canter**
   a. a metal container
   b. a type of lantern
   c. a slow, easy gallop

   SENTENCE: _____
   _____
   _____
   _____

Name: _____ Date: _____

The dictionary lists the part of speech of each entry word. But did you know that many words may be used as more than one part of speech?

Directions: Use a dictionary to help you answer each question.

THIS INFORMATION WILL HELP YOU, TOO!

noun: names a person, place, or thing. The abbreviation **n.** stands for *noun*.

verb: shows action. The abbreviation **v.** stands for *verb*.

adjective: describes a noun. The abbreviation **adj.** stands for *adjective*.

---

1. What is a **verb** definition of the word *finger?* _____

   _____

2. What part of speech is the word *muggy*, and what does the word mean?

   _____

3. Can the word *dog* be used as a **verb**? _____ If so, what is its meaning?

   _____

4. Can the word *cider* be used as a **verb**? _____ If so, what is its meaning?

   _____

5. What is an **adjective** definition of the word *blind?*

   _____

   _____

6. What is a **noun** definition of *blind?*

   _____

   _____

   _____

   _____

Name: _____   **Date:** _____

When you can't figure out a word's meaning on your own, turn to the dictionary!

Directions: First, guess the meaning of each **boldface** word in the paragraph. Write your guess. Then, look up the word in your dictionary and write that definition.

Going Down!

I boarded the elevator on the fifth floor of Mumson's Department Store. It began to go down. "Five, four, three," said the **digital** display above the door. Then, "Clunk!" The elevator **jolted** to a stop. Quickly, I pushed the **crimson** alarm button.

"We'll have you out of there in a **jiffy**," called a **savior** from above. With a **metallic** clatter, the elevator gears turned, and I began to move again.

1. **digital**

MY GUESS: _____

_____

_____

PER DICTIONARY: _____

_____

_____

2. **jolted**

MY GUESS: _____

_____

_____

PER DICTIONARY: _____

_____

_____

3. **crimson**

MY GUESS: _____

_____

_____

PER DICTIONARY: _____

_____

_____

4. **jiffy**

MY GUESS: _____

_____

_____

PER DICTIONARY: _____

_____

_____

5. **savior**

MY GUESS: _____

_____

_____

PER DICTIONARY: _____

_____

_____

6. **metallic**

MY GUESS: _____

_____

_____

PER DICTIONARY: _____

_____

_____

Name: _____   **Date:** _____

It's a good idea to check the dictionary to make sure that your spelling is accurate.

A. Directions: Some of the following words are spelled correctly. Some are misspelled. Put a **C** by the *correct* words. Put a **check (✓)** by the misspelled words. Rewrite the misspelled words correctly.

1. _____ baloons _____

2. _____ circus _____

3. _____ goverment _____

4. _____ diamond _____

5. _____ hammick _____

6. _____ photagraph _____

7. _____ treasure _____

8. _____ buckit _____

9. _____ pionear _____

10. _____ hamburger _____

11. _____ backwerds _____

12. _____ scientist _____

13. _____ villian _____

14. _____ violin _____

15. _____ gorilla _____

B. Directions: Use five words from above in sentences. Be sure to spell them correctly!

1. _____

2. _____

3. _____

4. _____

5. _____

Name: _____   **Date:** _____

Practice makes perfect! The next few pages will help you become a dictionary pro!

Directions: Use a dictionary to answer the following questions.

1. Which syllable is accented in the word *crispy*?

   _____

2. What part of speech is *delicious*?

   _____

3. Is *donut* correctly spelled?

   _____

4. Can *cue* be used as both a noun and a verb?

   _____

5. What is the noun meaning of *dove*?

   _____

6. How is *entertain* divided into syllables?

   _____

7. Can *beach* be used as a verb?

   _____

8. What is a *gibbon*?

   _____

   _____

   _____

9. How is *saxophone* divided into syllables?

   _____

10. Does the entry for *piano* have an illustration?

    _____

11. What is the definition of *shoddy*?

    _____

    _____

    _____

12. Can the word *fan* be used as both a noun and a verb?

    _____

Name: _____   **Date:** _____

A. Directions: A key word in each sentence is underlined. Write **T** if the statement is *true*. Write **F** if it is *false*. Use a dictionary to check your work.

1. _____ The word <u>fat</u> can be used as a verb.

2. _____ <u>Hunger</u> can be both a noun and a verb.

3. _____ <u>Hundred</u> is a three-syllable word.

4. _____ <u>Locket</u> is a verb meaning "to latch tightly."

5. _____ A <u>prawn</u> is a shellfish much like a large shrimp.

6. _____ The word <u>pray</u> would fall between the guide words *practice* and *preach*.

7. _____ <u>Accident</u> is a three-syllable word.

8. _____ The word <u>lap</u> has more than one meaning.

B. Directions: Write sentences using five of the underlined words above.

1. _____

_____

2. _____

_____

3. _____

_____

4. _____

_____

5. _____

_____

Name: _____   **Date:** _____

What a difference just one little letter can **b**ake!
No, no—I mean **c**ake! Or is it **f**ake or **l**ake? Or maybe
rake, **s**ake, **t**ake, **w**ake? Oh, yes, I remember now.
What a difference just one little letter can **MAKE**!

Directions: Change one letter in the **boldface** word to create a word that fits the sentence. Write the new word on the line. Use the first one as an example.

1. The suspect could not get out of jail until someone posted his **pail**. _____ *bail* _____

2. Chris decided to **mew** the lawn while the weather was dry. _____

3. The company paid females and **moles** equal salaries. _____

4. If you **seek** through that hole in the fence, you can see the house next door. _____

5. For every item we buy, we must pay a three percent sales **wax**. _____

6. A pirate's ghost is believed to **gaunt** the shipyards. _____

7. Jessie's pancakes are special because she puts apples in the **bitter**. _____

8. If you open the window, there will be a **drift**. _____

9. When Wally sleeps on his back, he **snares** loudly. _____

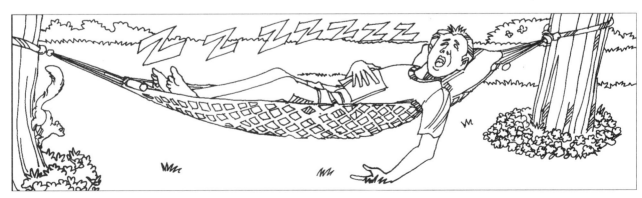

Name: _____   **Date:** _____

Can you recognize word groups? All the words—except one—in each group below have something in common!

Directions: Circle the word in each group that does *not* belong with the others. Then tell what the other words have in common. Use #1 as an example.

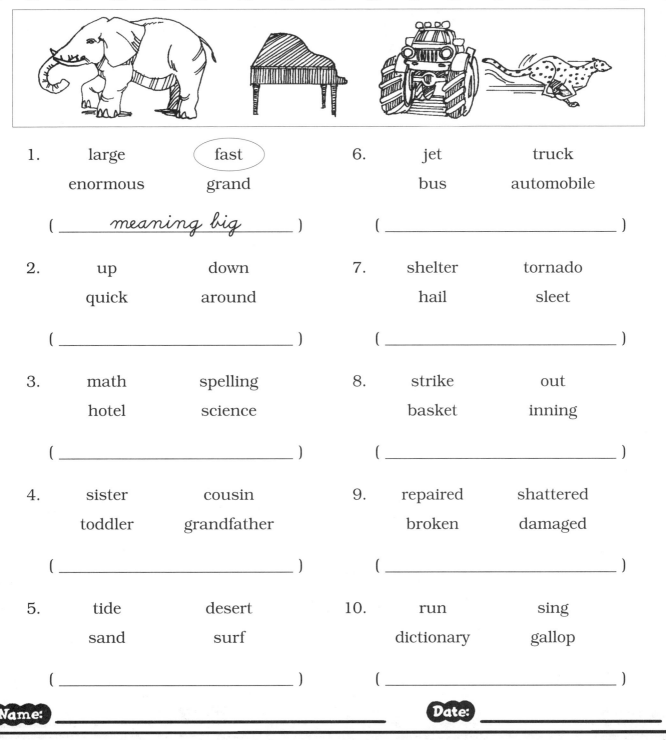

1. large   (fast)
   enormous   grand
   (____*meaning big*____)

6. jet   truck
   bus   automobile
   (_____)

2. up   down
   quick   around
   (_____)

7. shelter   tornado
   hail   sleet
   (_____)

3. math   spelling
   hotel   science
   (_____)

8. strike   out
   basket   inning
   (_____)

4. sister   cousin
   toddler   grandfather
   (_____)

9. repaired   shattered
   broken   damaged
   (_____)

5. tide   desert
   sand   surf
   (_____)

10. run   sing
    dictionary   gallop
    (_____)

Name: _____ **Date:** _____

> Most nouns are made plural by adding <u>s</u> or <u>es</u>. The plurals of some nouns, however, are formed by other spelling changes. Can you recognize *irregular* plural nouns?

A. **Directions:** Circle the plural noun in each sentence.

1. Dr. Eng, the dentist, has a painless way to pull teeth.

2. The books on the shelves are arranged in alphabetical order.

3. Seven people will fit comfortably in the van.

4. The pack of wolves howled in the frosty moonlight.

B. **Directions:** Circle the correctly spelled plural noun. Then use the word in a sentence.

1. calfs   calfes   calves

   _____

2. knives   knifes   kniven

   _____

3. meese   mice   mouses

   _____

4. thievs   thieves   thiefs

   _____

5. foots   feet   feat

   _____

Name: _____   **Date:** _____

Most plural nouns end in s—but there are exceptions!
If you're not sure how to write the plural form of a
noun correctly, check the dictionary.

Directions: The **boldface** noun in each sentence should be plural.
Write the correct plural form. Use a dictionary for help.

1. King Wapedopo came from a far-off land where men had
   many **wife** (_____).

2. The cat with nine **life** (_____) survived a fall from
   the roof and a spin in the clothes dryer.

3. At closing, the bakery gives away **loaf** (_____) of bread.

4. Kim couldn't decide which of the silk **scarf** (_____)
   she liked best.

5. Please cut that huge sandwich into two **half** (_____).

6. The autumn **leaf** (_____) made a colorful pile.

7. Three **woman** (_____)
   remodeled the old house.

8. The camel waited between the
   two **cactus** (_____).

9. A team of **ox** (_____)
   pulled the wagon.

10. The tale told of hundreds of tiny **elf**
    (_____) who cleaned
    the castle each night.

OUCH!

Name: _____   **Date:** _____

> *Slang* is a highly informal kind of language. Slang expressions go in and out of style. They're never used in serious speech or writing. Some examples of slang words for money are *moolah*, *bread*, and *dough*.

A. Directions: Match each slang term in the second column with its meaning in the first column. Write a letter by each number.

1. _____ clothes	a. nerd	
2. _____ man	b. duds	
3. _____ a fight	c. goof	
4. _____ cowardly	d. slammer	
5. _____ house	e. rumble	
6. _____ to tell on others	f. dude	
7. _____ prison	g. pad	
8. _____ one dollar bill	h. rat	
9. _____ mistake	i. chicken	
10. _____ someone dull	j. buck	

CHECK OUT THE DUDE IN THE COOL DUDS.

B. Directions: List three slang words that you and your friends use. Then write a sentence using each word you listed.

1. _____   2. _____   3. _____

SENTENCES:

1. _____

2. _____

3. _____

Name: _____   Date: _____

Words with similar dictionary definitions can have very different "emotional" meanings. People will react to the words differently. The emotional meanings of words are called *connotations* or *shades of meaning*.

EXAMPLE: *Slender* carries a positive meaning.
Skinny suggests something negative.

A. **Directions:** Circle the more *positive* word in each pair.

1. gentleman / fellow
2. demand / request
3. cautious / timid
4. weird / unusual
5. nosy / curious
6. heavy / fat

7. cheap / thrifty
8. complain / whine
9. silly / amusing
10. duties / chores
11. daring / reckless
12. toil / work

B. **Directions:** Write sentences using five of the words you circled above.

1. _____
_____

2. _____
_____

3. _____
_____

4. _____
_____

5. _____
_____

Name: _____ **Date:** _____

When choosing words, look beyond dictionary meanings. Think about the reactions people might have when they read or hear certain words.

A. Directions: Read each sentence. Put a plus (+) on the line if the **boldface** word has a *positive* connotation. Put a minus (–) on the line if the word has a *negative* connotation.

1. _____ Winnie's jokes are always **silly**.

2. _____ On the other hand, Sid's jokes are very **funny**.

3. _____ Jim **begged** Francie to go out on a date.

4. _____ Tony **invited** Sarah to the prom.

5. _____ Alex **chatted** with Sandra while waiting in the ticket line.

6. _____ Owen **jabbered** at me all through the movie.

B. Directions: Which description creates a more positive picture? Write the answer on the line.

1. Easygoing Ernie *or* Lazy Larry _____

2. Irresponsible Ira *or* Carefree Carla _____

3. Unique Monique *or* Odd Claude _____

4. Plain Paula *or* Natural Nellie _____

5. Naughty Nicky *or* Bad Brad _____

Name: _____   **Date:** _____

> *Euphemisms* are words or phrases that make something ordinary, unpleasant, or harsh seem better or more important.

EXAMPLE: *Old person* has a negative connotation.
Senior citizen has a positive connotation.

A. Directions: A euphemism in the box could replace each more direct word or phrase listed below. Write the euphemism on the correct line.

hairstylist	
beef	
intelligence agent	
pass away	
golden years	
visually impaired	
memorial service	
pre-owned vehicle	

1. die → _____
2. blind → _____
3. spy → _____
4. cow meat → _____
5. funeral → _____
6. barber → _____
7. old age → _____
8. used car → _____

B. Directions: Read the **boldface** euphemism in each sentence. Write its more direct meaning. An example has been done for you.

1. As Leslie's teacher, I must report that she sometimes **stretches the truth**. ___*tells lies*___

2. The prisoners were taken to the **house of correction**. _____

3. When it comes to schoolwork, Tiffany is an **underachiever**. _____

4. Mr. McGee is having trouble paying bills while he is **between jobs**. _____

Name: _____ **Date:** _____

Euphemisms **are words and phrases used to make something sound better or more pleasant. They are also used to cover up or soften the blunt facts.**

A. Directions: Match the following menu items with the common euphemisms on the right. Put a letter by each number. Use a dictionary for help.

1. _____ cow flesh   a. hamburger

2. _____ fish eggs   b. hot dog

3. _____ calf glands   c. poultry

4. _____ chicken meat   d. beef

5. _____ cow stomach   e. soda

6. _____ ground cow   f. caviar

7. _____ carbonated sugar water   g. tripe

8. _____ ground up animal parts   h. sweetbreads
       stuffed in a tube

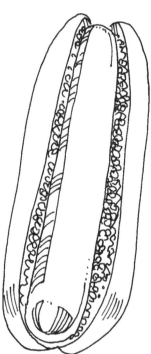

B. Directions: Rewrite the following sentences. Replace each **boldface** euphemism with more direct language.

1. I was sorry to hear that
   Mrs. Watson **lost her husband**. _____

2. All public buildings should have an
   entrance for the **physically disabled**. _____

3. Lester Lee was hired as a **custodial engineer**. _____

Name: _____   **Date:** _____

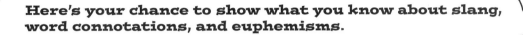

Here's your chance to show what you know about slang, word connotations, and euphemisms.

A. Directions: Circle a letter to correctly complete each statement.

1. *Slang* is
   a. informal language that is not used in serious writing.
   b. formal language used in reports and research papers.
   c. words or phrases that create negative feelings.

2. *C*onnotations are
   a. misspelled words.
   b. the feelings associated with certain words.
   c. dictionary definitions.

3. Word *connotations* are
   a. always positive.
   b. always negative.
   c. sometimes positive and sometimes negative.

4. A *euphemism* is a
   a. negative way of saying something.
   b. more pleasant way of saying something.
   c. foreign phrase.

B. Directions: Follow the directions to complete each item.

1. Write a sentence about a friend who wears nice clothes. Use at least one *slang* expression.

   _____

   _____

2. Imagine you're writing a sympathy note to a friend whose relative has died. Include a *euphemism* in your note.

   _____

   _____

3. Rewrite the following sentence. Replace the **boldface** words with words that have a more positive *connotation*.

   *Terry **toiled** in his garden all weekend because he is too **cheap** to hire help.*

   _____

   _____

Name: _____   **Date:** _____

Show your "word smarts" by making comparisons. An *analogy* compares things that are <u>alike</u> or <u>different</u> in some way.

SAMPLE ANALOGY: *Up* is to *down* as *left* is to *right*.

Directions: Complete each analogy with a word from the box.

cage	date	glove	green	lemon	pilot	hungry	junior	sad	walk

1. *Laugh* is to *happy* as *cry* is to _____.

2. *Sweet* is to *sugar* as *sour* is to _____.

3. *Water* is to *thirsty* as *food* is to _____.

4. *Old* is to *young* as *senior* is to _____.

5. *Fish* is to *bowl* as *bird* is to _____.

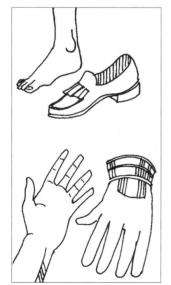

6. *Sing* is to *talk* as *dance* is to _____.

7. *Foot* is to *shoe* as *hand* is to _____.

8. *Train* is to *engineer* as *airplane* is to _____.

9. *Sky* is to *blue* as *grass* is to _____.

10. *Clock* is to *time* as *calendar* is to _____.

Name: _____   **Date:** _____

Increasing your ability to make comparisons makes your speech and writing much more interesting.

Directions: Decide which word makes sense in each sentence. Then circle the word that completes the analogy.

1. *Five* is to *ten* as *six* is to ___.

   seven   twelve   eighteen

2. *Pot* is to *pan* as *knife* is to ___.

   eat   food   fork

3. *Smart* is to *wise* as *dumb* is to ___.

   dull   brilliant   tall

4. *Tongue* is to *mouth* as *pupil* is to ___.

   face   body   eye

5. *Bear* is to *cub* as *deer* is to ___.

   doe   buck   fawn

6. *Skin* is to *bandage* as *tire* is to ___.

   rim   patch   flat

7. *Apple* is to *fruit* as *celery* is to ___.

   vegetable   crunchy   food

8. *Paintings* are to *museum* as *animals* are to ___.

   forest   zoo   people

9. *Fire* is to *burn* as *water* is to ___.

   wet   moisten   cold

10. *Mississippi* is to *River* as *Grand* is to ___.

   Huge   Canyon   Outstanding

Use the knowledge you've gained—as well as the clues—to solve this analogy crossword puzzle.

Directions: Write the missing word in each analogy on the puzzle.

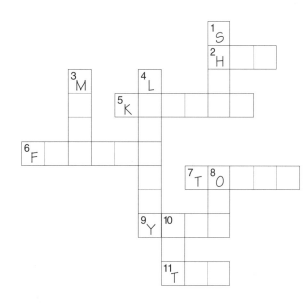

ACROSS

2. *Refrigerator* is to *cold* as *furnace* is to ___.

5. *Dog* is to *puppy* as *cat* is to ___.

6. *Bracelet* is to *wrist* as *ring* is to ___.

7. *Today* is to *yesterday* as *tomorrow* is to ___.

9. *Day* is to *week* as *month* is to ___.

11. *Three* is to *four* as *nine* is to ___.

DOWN

1. *Button* is to *coat* as *lace* is to ___.

3. *Day* is to *sun* as *night* is to ___.

4. *Money* is to *bank* as *book* is to ___.

8. *Speedboat* is to *motor* as *rowboat* is to ___.

10. *Bedroom* is to *sleep* as *kitchen* is to ___.

Name: _____   Date: _____

Abbreviations are commonly used short forms of words, such as *U.S.A.* for *United States of America*. You will often use abbreviations in your own writing.

A. Directions: Circle the most common meaning of each **boldface** abbreviation. Use the dictionary for help.

1. **B.A.**   Bachelor of Arts   before arrival   Best Actor

2. **D.A.**   date of arrival   District Attorney   don't answer

3. **ea.**   eager   each   early

4. **Jan.**   janitor   Junior   January

5. **FDA**   Food and Drug Administration   Future Democrats of America
   Federal Department of Agriculture

6. **Co.**   copilot   Company   cousin

7. **Sr.**   Senior   Senator   Secret Service

8. **Mon.**   moon   money   Monday

9. **ASAP**   Americans Supporting All People   as soon as possible
   Association for Special Athletic Pursuits

10. **tbsp.**   table tennis   track sprinter   tablespoon

B. Directions: List three abbreviations that you've seen. Then write their meanings.

ABBREVIATION	MEANING
1. _____	_____
2. _____	_____
3. _____	_____

Name: _____   **Date:** _____

Be on the lookout for abbreviations as you read. If you don't know their meaning, check a dictionary.

Directions: Circle the abbreviations in the following sentences. Then write the meanings of the abbreviations you circled.

1. On Nov. 1, Gina starts her sales clerk job.

   _____

2. Sheri, a volunteer in Dr. Bittner's office, wants to be a nurse.

   _____

3. Thomas hopes to someday be known as Capt. Conrad, commander of a huge ship.

   _____

4. Julio would love to report the news for NBC.

   _____

5. Sophie found a summer job in Washington, D.C.

   _____

6. Because Emma loves numbers, she would like to work for the IRS.

   _____

7. Leo wants to join the FBI when he graduates from college.

   _____

Name: _____   **Date:** _____

Have some fun with this bountiful bonanza of bodacious "B" words.

Directions: Study each illustration below. Then write a couple of sentences that could be the picture caption. For each caption, use two or more of the "B" words in the box.

| background | balance | beach | bench | bicyclist | blanket |
| border | borrow | bounce | breeze | bubble | buddy |

1. AT THE PARK: _____

_____

_____

_____

_____

_____

2. THEATER LOBBY: _____

_____

_____

_____

_____

_____

3. BEACH PARTY: _____

_____

_____

_____

_____

_____

Name: _____   **Date:** _____

The English language is full of "borrowed" words that come to us from other languages. Do you recognize some of the Spanish words on this page?

Directions: The **boldface** word in each sentence entered our language through Spanish. Circle a letter to show the correct meaning of the word. Use a dictionary as needed.

1. Mr. Vincente asked me to join the family for lunch on their **patio**.

   a. large wheat ranch

   b. paved, outdoor area next to house

2. Lucio Vincente will ride in next week's **rodeo**.

   a. auto race

   b. contest of cowboy skills

3. Sound bounced off the **canyon** walls.

   a. long, narrow valley

   b. large, empty building

4. The barn is south of the garden and north of the **corral**.

   a. fenced place for animals

   b. main farmhouse

5. The **burro** had long, furry ears.

   a. puppy   b. donkey

6. When the theater doors open, there could be a **stampede**.

   a. rush of people or animals in the same direction

   b. cool breeze blowing in

Name: _____   **Date:** _____

Do you know *why* different holidays are celebrated? It helps if you understand the words in their names!

A. Directions: Match the **boldface** word with its meaning. Write a letter by each number.

1. _____ **Memorial** Day

2. _____ **Independence** Day

3. _____ **Veterans** Day

4. _____ New Year's **Eve**

5. _____ **Labor** Day

a. freedom from the control of others

b. having to do with work or workers

c. the evening before a special day

d. those who have served in the armed forces

e. something meant to honor or remember people

B. Directions: Write several sentences about one of the holidays listed above. Tell when it is and how it's celebrated. (You can get information in the dictionary or an encyclopedia.)

_____

_____

_____

_____

_____

_____

_____

_____

_____

_____

_____

_____

Name: _____ **Date:** _____

> Let's review some words that are commonly used in place of family names.

A. Directions: Write the correct word from the box on each line.

| father-in-law | aunt | cousin | great-grandmother | stepbrother | spouse | stepfather | uncle |

1. Bridget is my mother's sister. She is my _____.

2. Shane is my mother's brother. He is my _____.

3. Peter is my mother's father. He is my father's _____.

4. Ramon is Aunt Bridget's son. He is my _____.

5. Ella is my grandmother's mother. She is my _____.

6. Steven Parker married Sara Holmes. Sara already has a daughter, Iris. Steve has become Iris's _____.

7. Steve also has a son, Willie. Willie is Iris's _____.

8. Sara has become Steve's wife, or _____.

B. Directions: Read the first sentence. Then circle a word to complete the second sentence.

1. Next month, Tim's father will marry Megan's mother. Tim will be Megan's (cousin / stepbrother).

2. Mom's sister has a son named Troy. Troy is Mom's (nephew / niece).

3. Mom and Dad's three kids include Mark, Byron, and me. The three of us are (cousins / siblings).

4. Mom's brother Perry married Lisa. Lisa is Mom's (aunt / sister-in-law).

5. My oldest relative is my grandfather's father. He is my (great-grandfather / father-in-law).

Name: _____   **Date:** _____

When do you capitalize a "family relationship" word?
Only when it's used as a name or part of a name.

A. Directions: Put three lines under all letters that should be capitalized. Some sentences will *not* need corrections. Use the first sentence as an example.

1. Bob and dad left for their camping trip.

2. They are using uncle Grant's tent.

3. Bob, my uncle, is an experienced camper.

4. My father, on the other hand, has never slept in a tent.

5. I was invited to join them on the trip, and so was cousin Ralph.

6. Ralph and I, however, decided not to join our fathers.

7. We will spend the weekend with Rita, Ralph's mother.

8. While uncle Bob and dad are in a cold tent, cousin Ralph and I will sit in a warm kitchen eating aunt Rita's hot apple pie!

B. Directions: Write two or three sentences about your family. Use at least three words that name family relationships. Check word capitalization carefully.

_____

_____

_____

_____

_____

_____

Name: _____   **Date:** _____

Experience this exercise with all five of your senses!

A. **Directions:** Think about the items listed in the box. Classify each item under the sense you'd use most in observing it.

a doorbell	a warm breeze	some sugar	a burn	salt
a gas leak	a photograph	a melody	a rainbow	perfume

SMELL: _____   _____

HEAR: _____   _____

TASTE: _____   _____

SEE: _____   _____

FEEL: _____   _____

B. **Directions:** On the blank line, write the sense *(sight, hearing, taste, smell,* or *touch)* that relates to each word. The first one has been done for you. Use a dictionary as needed.

1. delicious ____*taste*____

2. stinky _____

3. fragrant _____

4. attractive _____

5. musical _____

6. slippery _____

7. sour _____

8. soft _____

9. ugly _____

10. prickly _____

11. chirping _____

12. spicy _____

Name: _____   **Date:** _____

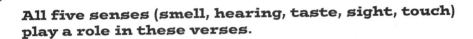

**All five senses (smell, hearing, taste, sight, touch)
play a role in these verses.**

Directions: Unscramble the letters to complete each verse with a rhyming word.
Then answer the question or questions that follow each verse.

1. One taste that gives your mouth a tickle,

   Is the sweet and sour of a juicy **(KILCEP)** _____.

   Which two words in the verse describe *tastes*?

   _____   _____

2. Wailing sirens, screeching brakes,

   Those are the sounds an accident **(SAMEK)** _____.

   Which two words in the verse describe *sounds*?

   _____   _____

3. The sun above so bright and warm

   Makes the world seem safe from **(MAHR)** _____.

   Which word describes something you *feel*? _____

   What word relates to *sight*? _____

4. The soup is bubbling in the pot.

   Don't touch the handle! It is too **(THO)** _____.

   Which word describes a *sound*? _____

   Which word describes something you *feel*? _____

5. The fans stomped their feet and gave a roar!

   At last, their team had tied the **(CORSE)** _____.

   Which two words create *sounds*?

   _____   _____

Name: _____   **Date:** _____

Sometimes it's easy to see why people and pets are called by certain nicknames.

A. Directions: Some popular pet names are listed below. Write a sentence describing an animal that would be likely to be given each name.

1. Snowball: _____

_____

2. Fluffy: _____

_____

3. Tweetie: _____

_____

4. Princess: _____

_____

5. Buddy: _____

6. Bubbles: _____

7. King: _____

B. Directions: People can have descriptive nicknames too! What type of person does each nickname suggest to you?

1. Tex: _____

2. Gramps: _____

3. Red: _____

4. Junior: _____

Name: _____   Date: _____

Have you ever heard someone called a "Scrooge"? Certain names from literature, history, or the Bible suggest particular traits and qualities. A dictionary can help you understand these references.

A. **Directions:** Match each name on the left with a trait it suggests. Use a dictionary as needed.

1. _____ Scrooge   a. wise

2. _____ Methuselah   b. strong

3. _____ Benedict Arnold   c. disloyal

4. _____ Hercules   d. cheap

5. _____ Solomon   e. old

B. **Directions:** What are people saying about Bob? Circle the letter of the answer.

1. Bob is such a Romeo!

   This means that Bob . . .
   a. is a great athlete!
   b. has a way with the girls!

2. My boss, Bob, is a Simon Legree!

   This means that Bob is . . .
   a. very kind to his employees!
   b. a cruel taskmaster!

3. Bob has the Midas touch!

   This means that Bob . . .
   a. makes lots of money!
   b. plays the piano very well!

4. Compared to his friend Sam, Bob is a Goliath!

   This means that Bob is . . .
   a. a really big guy!
   b. extremely smart!

Name: _____ **Date:** _____

"**Mabel Mumford runs like a gazelle,**" **a sports reporter wrote. That kind of comparison is called a** *figure of speech.* **It creates a clear picture.**

A. Directions: Read each sentence. Underline the two things being compared. The first one has been done for you.

1. The <u>rain</u> fell on the dry fields like a <u>welcome stranger</u>.

2. The ambulance light flashed as red as blood.

3. The athlete's body was a well-tuned machine.

4. Saturday is my best friend!

5. Clara's yellow purse looked like a big banana.

6. Hal carried his problem around like a giant weight.

7. Her smile was as bright as an upside-down rainbow.

8. The melted candy bar looked as tasty as a mud puddle.

9. The rumor spread through the school like a case of the flu.

10. The dancers in colorful costumes swayed like wildflowers in the wind.

B. Directions: Complete each sentence by making a comparison. You can use words from the box below or come up with ideas of your own.

clacking typewriter keys	squirrels	bees	ants	kangaroos	diamonds	tears	ox	a horse

1. The excited children hopped about the room like _____.

2. The raindrops glitter like _____.

3. Like _____, the carpenters worked busily all day long.

4. After working out at the gym, Jason feels as strong as an _____.

5. "Pat, tap, pat!" The sleet rapped against the house like _____
_____.

Name: _____ **Date:** _____

Writers sometimes draw comparisons to make a point.
These figures of speech help readers "get the picture."

Directions: Read the story and underline figures of speech. Then list the things the writer compares. The first one has been done for you.

It was a hot afternoon. <u>Like a furnace, the wind blasted heat.</u> Pavement sizzled like a stove top, cooking the soles of my shoes. What a day to begin my job as a painter's helper!

Ms. Delilo watched from inside the house. She nodded approval as we began work. A color like rich coffee with cream soon coated one section. I stood back and admired my work. Sweat rolled down my face like a waterfall—but I was proud. My first paint job was as perfect as an A+ test score!

Ms. Delilo came out. In the pitcher of lemonade she carried, ice cubes tinkled like bells.

"Put on your hat!" she told me. "Your sunburned face makes you look like a strawberry ice cream cone!"

1. _____wind_____ → _____furnace_____

2. _____ → _____

3. _____ → _____

4. _____ → _____

5. _____ → _____

6. _____ → _____

7. _____ → _____

Name: _____ **Date:** _____

Here's a chance to work with words that come from other languages.

A. **Directions:** The **boldface** word in each sentence is from another language. Write a modern English word from the box that now replaces the foreign word. (The word's origin is listed under it.)

market	neighbor	out	bus	proud	automobile

1. Today, my brother Mark bought his first **autos mobilis** _____.
   (LATIN)

2. Until today, Mark had taken the **omnibus** _____
   (LATIN)
   everywhere he went.

3. Mark bought his 1980 Ford from our next-
   door **heah gebur** _____.
   (OLD ENGLISH)

4. Now Mark can pick up groceries at the
   mercatus _____.
   (LATIN)

5. Mark is very **prud** _____ of his new set of wheels!
   (OLD ENGLISH)

6. He spends much of his time **ut** _____ on the driveway
   (OLD ENGLISH)
   polishing the paint.

B. **Directions:** Look up the following words in the dictionary. Write what you learn about the origin of each word.

1. July: _____

2. sandwich: _____

3. March: _____

4. Monday: _____

Name: _____ **Date:** _____

Certain Latin and Greek word parts are used in many English words. Knowing these common Greek and Latin roots can help you figure out word meanings.

LATIN

aqua = water
bi = two
annus = year

GREEK

tri = three
tele = at a distance
geos = earth

Directions: The hidden words below have Greek and Latin roots. Find and circle them in the puzzle. The words may go up, down, backward or forward. Check off each word as you find it in the puzzle.

____ AQUARIUM	
____ BICYCLE	
____ TRIANGLE	
____ TRIPLETS	
____ TRIO	
____ TELEPHONE	
____ TELEVISION	
____ GEOGRAPHY	
____ ANNUAL	
____ ANNIVERSARY	

```
D A H C S Y A B R X P
G O A Q U A R I U M O
E P L I S M G C E E H
O T L T T A P Y Z N J
G W E R O A R C I O Q
R T R I A N G L E H U
A M Y P K E A E N P R
P A R L A U N N A E T
H C E E C H L G I L V
Y I B T R I O R O E B
N O I S I V E L E T C
A N N I V E R S A R Y
```

Name: _____   **Date:** _____

You might be surprised to find how many English words have Latin and Greek roots! Practice using some of them now.

Directions: The following words are from the puzzle on the last lesson. Underline the Greek or Latin root in each word. Then write a sentence using the word. The first one has been done for you. A dictionary can help you with word meanings.

1. <u>aqua</u>rium: *I love to watch the otters at the Monterey Bay Aquarium.*

2. bicycle: _____

3. triangle: _____

4. triplets: _____

5. trio: _____

6. telephone: _____

7. television: _____

8. geography: _____

9. annual: _____

10. anniversary: _____

Name: _____   **Date:** _____

Boost your knowledge of the past by learning some common historical terms.

A. **Directions:** Write a letter to match each **boldface** term with its meaning. If you need help, check a dictionary.

1. _____ **century**

2. _____ **civil war**

3. _____ **colony**

4. _____ **decade**

5. _____ **revolution**

6. _____ **dictator**

a. 10 years

b. 100 years

c. a fight for a change in government

d. a settlement that is ruled by another country

e. a ruler who has complete power

f. a war in which two parts of a country fight each other

B. **Directions:** Fill in the blanks with the words listed above to complete the paragraphs. Use the first letter of each word as a clue.

A BRIEF HISTORY OF WAGANALAND

For 100 years, the people of Waganaland dreamed of freedom. Throughout that c_____ their tiny country was ruled by General Bigshotman. This powerful d_____ controlled not only Waganaland but also its c_____ of settlers across the sea.

One day, a strong leader rose up and called for a war to change the government. The r_____ began in 1910 and lasted until 1920. Then, after a d_____ of fighting, a new government took control. Waganaland was at peace until 1994, when a c_____ w_____ broke out between the Waganalanders of the East and those of the West.

Name: _____   **Date:** _____

All citizens should understand the workings of their government. Do you know the language of government?

A. Directions: Write a letter to match the **boldface** term with its meaning. If you need help, check a dictionary.

1. _____ **election**
2. _____ **candidate**
3. _____ **ballot**
4. _____ **citizens**
5. _____ **constitution**
6. _____ **vote**
7. _____ **campaign**

a. a list of choices on which people mark their pick

b. those who live in a community and have rights and responsibilities

c. the process of choosing candidates by voting

d. to show your choice; to say what you think should happen

e. a planned effort to get people to choose a certain candidate

f. an official, written plan of government

g. a person running for office

MY FELLOW CITIZENS...

DEBA
CON
DIS

B. Directions:

Complete the following speech by filling in the blanks with words listed above. Use the first letter of each word as a clue.

A C_____ **Speaks**

My fellow c_____,
I speak to you on the eve of this
important e_____.
I ask you to v_____ for me.
Tonight my long c_____
ends. You've heard my plans and
promises. Tomorrow, each of you

will put your b_____ in
the box. If I am elected, I promise to
uphold the c_____
of our country and do my very best to
enforce its laws!

Here are some words you'll need to know when you're talking about geography.

A. Directions: Write a letter to match each **boldface** term with its meaning. If you need help, check a dictionary.

1. _____ **border**   a. a place with water deep enough for ships to dock

2. _____ **climate**   b. a round model of the earth

3. _____ **population**   c. the typical kind of weather in a certain place

4. _____ **port**   d. the land bordering the sea

5. _____ **globe**   e. the total number of people who live in a place

6. _____ **coast**   f. line on a map that divides one state or
                                country from another

B. Directions: Complete the following paragraphs. Fill in the blanks with words listed above. Use the first letter of each word as a clue.

Where in the World?

"Where should we go on our trip?" Sonia asked Sammy. She spun a _g_____ and pointed to different cities. At last her finger came to rest along the _b_____ between Canada and the United States. "Should we leave the country?" she asked.

"We could sail along the western _c_____ and stop at a Canadian _p_____," Sammy suggested. "I've heard that the city of Vancouver, British Columbia, is an interesting place. It has a large _p_____ of people from all over the world. It also has a mild _c_____. People say it's not too hot and not too cold!"

> Our world is made up of people from many different cultures. Here are some words to know as we learn more about each other.

A. Directions: The following **boldface** words have to do with the study of world cultures. Beside each word, write the letter of its definition. If you need help, check a dictionary.

1. _____ **custom**

2. _____ **immigrants**

3. _____ **legends**

4. _____ **ancestors**

5. _____ **artifacts**

6. _____ **religion**

a. found objects that were used by people of the past

b. stories handed down through the years

c. a group of people's usual way of doing something

d. members of a person's family who lived long ago

e. a set of beliefs about God or a group of gods

f. people who come to a country to live there

B. Directions: Fill in the blanks with the words listed above to complete the following paragraph. Use the first letter of each word as a clue.

A Matter of Respect

Lu Quan and her family are among the many Chinese _i_____ who have come to the United States. The family brought traditions from China. One _c_____ is that of showing respect for elders. This is an important principle of Buddhism, a major _r_____ in China.

The Chinese people honor their _a_____. They feel they owe much to family members who came before them. Chinese _l_____ have been handed down from parents to children. They tell tales of grandparents who were very wise. Ancient carvings, paintings, and many other Chinese _a_____ show older people in respected roles.

Name: _____ **Date:** _____

You've probably heard that practice makes perfect. Try using some social studies terms that you've already studied.

Directions: The words in the "book" below are from lesson pages 117 through 120. Use each word to complete a sentence.

artifacts	immigrants
ballot	legend
border	population
climate	port
coast	revolution

1. Luis brought his family to live and work in America. Luis and his family are _____.

2. In 1776, American colonists fought for self-rule. The _____ began in 1776.

3. People from many parts of the world have a _____ about a great flood that swept the land.

4. In the distant future, people may look at a computer, an automobile, or an electric guitar as _____ of our civilization.

5. The treaty allowed free trade across the _____ between Mexico and the United States.

6. When gold was discovered, the _____ of California grew rapidly.

7. Each voter can voice an opinion by casting a _____.

8. When storms hit the Pacific _____, strong winds and rain can topple trees and knock out power.

9. Even though the _____ is cold and wet, tourists come to watch the winter storms.

10. The ship docked at its final _____ of call.

Name: _____ **Date:** _____

Building Vocabulary Skills and Strategies, Level 3 • Saddleback Publishing, Inc. ©2004 • 3 Watson, Irvine, CA 92618 • Phone (888) SDL-BACK • www.sdlback.com   121

Get ready to work with some words that might be helpful in your science class! As members of the animal world, we should all know these terms.

A. Directions: Complete each sentence with one of the words from the box. Use a dictionary as needed.

behave	cell	mammal	prey	skeleton	species

1. A _____ is a group of animals, including humans, that are alike in certain important ways.

2. A _____ is the basic unit of living matter.

3. Together, all the bones in a body make up a _____.

4. A _____ is a warm-blooded animal that has a backbone.

5. To act a certain way is to _____ that way.

6. An animal that is killed for food is called _____.

B. Directions: Now use the information you've learned. Circle the word that correctly completes each sentence.

1. Your backbone is a part of your (cell / skeleton).

2. A mouse is likely to be an eagle's (species / prey).

3. Monkeys and humans are both (mammals / cells).

4. Scientists look through microscopes to study (cells / prey).

5. Spaniels and poodles both belong to the canine (skeleton / species).

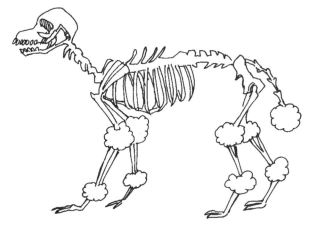

Name: _____   Date: _____

Here are some words you'll be likely to meet as you study our planet Earth.

A. **Directions:** Complete each sentence with one of the words from the box. Use a dictionary as needed.

erode	fault	glacier	smog	volcano

1. A _____ is an opening in the earth's surface through which melted rock is thrown up.

2. A huge body of ice that slowly moves across the land is called a _____.

3. A _____ is a very deep crack in the earth.

4. As it goes into the air, waste material from burning things is called _____.

5. Earth and rock are said to _____ as they slowly wear away.

B. **Directions:** Use information from Part A to answer each question.

1. Which is hotter, a glacier or a volcano? _____

2. If you came across a fault, would you be more likely to climb it or fall in it? _____

3. Which would be more likely to cause smog, a forest fire or a flood? _____

4. If your yard were eroding, would you be gaining ground or losing ground? _____

5. Long ago, Earth went through an ice age. During that period, would there have been glaciers or smog? _____

Name: _____ **Date:** _____

Will today's weather be dreary or bright? Climate conditions make a big difference to all of us. That's why it's important to know the vocabulary of weather.

A. Directions: Complete the crossword puzzle with the "weather words" in the box. The clues will help you select the correct words.

cloud	fog	hail	humidity	forecast	degrees

DOWN

1. a report of what the weather is likely to be

ACROSS

1. a large group of tiny water drops that float close to the ground, forming a thick mist

2. a large group of tiny water drops that float together in the sky

3. units used to measure amounts of heat in the air

4. balls of frozen ice that drop from the sky

5. the amount of water vapor (dampness) in the air

1.

1. _F_ _ _

2. _ _ _ _ _

3. _ _ _ _ _ _ _

4. _ _ _ _

5. _ _ _ _ _ _ _

B. Directions: Write a forecast for tomorrow's weather in your region. Use some of the words from the puzzle and other weather words you know.

_____

_____

_____

_____

_____

The *media* include all sources of news and entertainment. Do you get your information from a newspaper, television, or radio? Whichever you prefer, these words can help you keep up to date.

A. Directions: Write a letter to match each **boldface** term with its meaning. If you need help, check a dictionary.

1. _____ **headline**

2. _____ **reporter**

3. _____ **network**

4. _____ **broadcast**

5. _____ **feature**

6. _____ **editorial**

7. _____ **interview**

a. to send over the air by means of radio or television

b. an article or presentation that gives an opinion

c. a person who presents the news and often gathers and writes it too

d. words in large print at the top of a news story; they tell what the story is about

e. a chain of radio or TV stations that air many of the same programs

f. a meeting at which a person is questioned by a reporter

g. a special article or presentation

B. Directions: Circle the word that correctly completes each sentence.

1. All stations will (editorial / broadcast) the president's speech tonight.

2. The TV announcement said, "The following (headline / editorial) presents the opinion of this station."

3. A (network / headline) in the local paper read, "DOG HERO SAVES FAMILY FROM FIRE."

4. A report of the rescue was the (feature / reporter) story on the noon news.

5. Every newspaper (reporter / editorial) in town wrote about the story.

6. Timmy Lane, the dog's owner, appeared on NBC, a major television (reporter / network).

7. In a TV (network / interview), Timmy said his family members owed their lives to Barney, the brave little beagle.

Name: _____   **Date:** _____

> Whether you're at the supermarket or the mall, knowing certain words can help you shop wisely.

Directions: Read the following story. Think about the meaning of the **boldface** words. Then circle the correct word choice in each sentence.

Shopping Day

Saturday morning, Fritzie and Frank went to the supermarket. They always go early, when the store is less crowded. Frank likes to be one of the first **customers** of the day.

"Let's get this soap," Fritzie said as she and Frank pushed a cart through the aisles. She pointed to a sign that announced a 20 percent **discount**.

Frank pulled a **coupon** from his pocket. "This will give us 50 cents off!"

At the checkout counter, the **clerk** scanned the **bar code** on each item in

Frank and Fritzie's basket. When she rang up the sale, she exclaimed, "You got a real **bargain** today!"

1. *Customers* are people who are (parking their cars / buying things).

2. A *discount* is an amount (taken off / added to) a price.

3. A *coupon* is a ticket or piece of paper that (gives the holder special rights / can be used as identification).

4. A *clerk* will (sell / buy) things in the store.

5. The *bar code* on each item is a set of printed lines. When electronically read, these lines give (a list of ingredients / the price).

6. When the clerk said the soap was a *bargain*, she meant it was (extremely high in quality / at a lower-than-usual price).

Name: _____   **Date:** _____

A shopping trip can be fun, tiring, frustrating, exciting, or challenging. How do *you* feel about shopping?

Directions: Write a paragraph telling about one shopping trip that stands out from all the rest. Did you get a great bargain? Did you have an interesting or embarrassing experience? Did you meet someone unusual? In your paragraph, use at least three of these "marketplace" words: *customers, discount, coupon, clerk, bar code, bargain.*

_____

_____

_____

_____

_____

_____

_____

_____

_____

_____

_____

Name: _____   **Date:** _____

Learning these words can help you stay healthy:
contagious, diet, emergency, exercise, first aid, virus.

A. Directions: Complete each sentence with a word from the box. Use the clues in parentheses to help you select the correct word.

contagious	diet	emergency	exercise	first aid	virus

1. Juana caught a _____ (germ) that multiplies in living cells and causes disease.

2. Juana's illness was _____ (quickly spread from person to person).

3. Regular _____ (active use of the body) helps fight off illness.

4. Plan your _____ (what you usually eat and drink) carefully, keeping good health in mind.

5. Oh, no! There's been an accident, and it's an _____ (event that calls for action right away)!

6. At the accident scene, Brett gives the injured people _____ (help) while waiting for the ambulance.

B. Directions: Choose one of the following topics and circle it. Then write a few sentences about it. Use at least two words from the box in Part A.

TOPIC CHOICES

I've never been so sick!

How I stay healthy

How I saved the day

Everyone seems to have it!

The time I yelled "Help!"

_____
_____
_____
_____
_____
_____
_____

Name: _____   **Date:** _____

Here's a chance to do some original work using some of the words you've studied.

Directions: A good news story answers five questions. It tells *who, what, when, where,* and *why*. Put yourself in the role of reporter and answer those questions about a newsworthy happening. It can be a real or imagined event. Use at least five of the words below in your answers. Then write a headline for your story.

campaign	citizens	customers	vote	degrees
emergency	first aid	population	virus	volcano
interview	climate	contagious	smog	clerk

HEADLINE: _____

WHO? _____

WHAT? _____

WHEN? _____

WHERE? _____

WHY? _____

Name: _____   **Date:** _____

Whether you'd rather play a sport or watch one, here are some words to know.

Directions: First, complete the sentences with words from the box. Then, add the words to the puzzle, printing one letter on each short line. The answer to the riddle reads from top to bottom.

cheer	court	field	goal	opponent	practice	score	team

RIDDLE: *Call me the winner, the victor, the one who stands tall!*
Whatever you call me, I've beaten them all! Who am I?

1. The crowd was tense when the _____ was tied at seven to seven.

2. Fans began to _____ loudly as Mario Gomez came off the bench.

3. Hurrah! Mario scored a _____!

4. Now it looked like the home _____ was about to win the game.

5. Mario's hard work and months of _____ finally paid off.

6. Mario ran down the soccer _____, kicking the ball in front of him.

7. Next season, fans will see Mario on the basketball _____.

8. Mario faced every _____ he came up against with a friendly smile!

I am a →

1. _ _ _ _ _
2. _ _ _ _ _
3. _ _ _ _
4. _ _ _ _
5. _ _ _ _ _ _ _ _
6. _ _ _ _ _
7. _ _ _ _ _
8. _ _ _ _ _ _ _ _

Name: _____   Date: _____

The musical world owes much of its vocabulary to the Italian language. Here are just a few words: *solo, duet, opera, piano, violin, soprano, tempo, trombone, bravo*.

Directions: Complete the story with words from the box. You've been given the first letter of each word as a hint.

duet	opera	piano	violin	soprano	tempo	trombone	bravo	solo

The Performance

The lights dimmed as Ms. Condon's music class began its show. Kenny stood on the stage alone. He lifted his bow and slowly pulled it across the strings of his
v_____.
"Squawk!"

Kenny frowned and began again. This time, a sweet note filled the air. At the end of his
s_____, Kenny took a bow.

Next, two students came on stage. They were Mimi and Sid singing a
d_____. Mimi sang high in a sweet s_____ voice. When she hit her highest note, the audience gasped.

"Her voice is just amazing!" someone cried out. "She is sure to be an o_____ star someday!"

Umeko was the next performer. Her fingers seemed to fly over the black and white keys of the grand
p_____.
We noticed that she tapped her foot to the t_____ of the tune she played.

Finally, little Stevie came out. The tiny boy lifted a big, brass horn to his lips. He could barely reach far enough to pull the slide of the t_____ in and out.

"B_____!" shouted the audience at the end of the show.

It's time to do some more work with those musical words that came to us from Italy.

Directions: Write definitions of the words from the last lesson. Use the context of the story and a dictionary for help.

1. **bravo:** _____
_____
_____
_____

2. **duet:** _____
_____

3. **opera:** _____
_____

4. **piano:** _____
_____

5. **solo:** _____
_____

6. **soprano:** _____
_____

7. **tempo:** _____
_____

8. **trombone:** _____
_____

9. **violin:** _____
_____

Name: _____   **Date:** _____

Let's take a look at a restaurant menu. Make sure you recognize words you'll need to use when dining out.

Directions: Georgio's Cafe is offering the following menu this evening. Read it over. Then match each **boldface** word with its meaning. Use a dictionary as needed.

Georgio's

APPETIZERS
Crab and Herb Ravioli
Spicy Shrimp

ENTREES
(served a la carte)
Lamb Chops
Vegetarian Pasta
Fillet of Beef

SOUP and SALAD
Chopped Cabbage Slaw
Soup du Jour

DESSERTS
Apple Tart
Ice Cream Sundae

BEVERAGES
Coffee, Tea, Juices

1. _____ **appetizer**

2. _____ **herb**

3. _____ **ravioli**

4. _____ **slaw**

5. _____ **beverages**

6. _____ **du jour**

7. _____ **a la carte**

8. _____ **chops**

9. _____ **vegetarian**

10. _____ **pasta**

11. _____ **fillet**

12. _____ **tart**

13. _____ **sundae**

a. drinks

b. special of the day

c. a bit of food served to start a meal

d. slices of meat cut with a piece of bone

e. having a separate price for each menu item

f. pocket of dough, usually filled with meat or cheese

g. a lean piece of meat without any bones

h. ice cream covered with syrup, fruit, nuts, etc.

i. salad made of shredded vegetables

j. a small pie, usually filled with fruit or jam

k. made of grains, vegetables, and fruits; suited for those who choose to eat no meat

l. dough that is shaped and often dried to form types of noodles; any dish containing these noodles

m. a special plant, such as mint or parsley, used as seasoning

A. Directions: Welcome to Georgio's! Reread the menu in the last lesson. Then imagine that you are dining out as a restaurant critic. Write a short review describing your meal at Georgio's.

_____

_____

_____

_____

_____

B. Directions: Whether you're dining out or eating in, here are six more terms to know. Complete each sentence with a word from the simmering pot. The words in parentheses will help you make the right choice.

sautéed
grilled   roasted
simmered
poached   blended
deep-fried

1. Carrots are good _____ (fried quickly in a pan with very little fat).

2. A stew should be slowly _____ (cooked just below the boiling point for several hours).

3. A fine piece of beef is best _____ (cooked in an oven with little or no liquid) with a little salt and pepper.

4. Fish and chips are _____ (cooked in a deep pan of boiling fat or oil) until they're crisp.

5. Vegetables for the soup were _____ (chopped and whirled until they turned into a well-mixed liquid) in the food processor.

6. The chicken was _____ (cooked on a metal grate over a hot fire) until it was brown and crisp outside and moist inside.

7. Some people like eggs _____ (cooked in lightly boiling water) and served over toast.

Name: _____ Date: _____

Now that you've s-t-r-e-t-c-h-e-d your vocabulary, put your word skills to the test.

Directions: Answer each question to show what you've learned.

1. Is *answer* or *request* a synonym for *ask*? _____

2. Is a *ballot* or *ballet* a dance? _____

3. Which is a compound word— *basket* or *basketball*? _____

4. What is the base word of *payment*? _____

5. What is the plural form of *mouse*? _____

6. To you, who is the child of your uncle or aunt? _____

7. How is a person related to his or her spouse? _____

8. How many syllables are there in the word *customer*? _____

9. Which syllable is accented in the word *neighbor*? _____

10. What does the abbreviation *Nov.* stand for? _____

11. Of the words *super* and *supper*, which means "really great"? _____

12. What is a homonym of the word *sundae*? _____

13. Is *glad* or *afraid* an antonym of *sad*? _____

14. The word *athlete* is what part of speech? _____

15. What is the base word of *happiness*? _____

16. What is the contraction for the words *should not*? _____

17. Which sails the seas—a *sloop* or a *slop*? _____

18. Would you hear a *buzz* or taste it? _____

Name: _____ **Date:** _____

Complete this **POWER PUZZLE** and you're quickly becoming a *wizard* with words!

Directions: Use the clues to help you complete the crossword puzzle.

ACROSS

1. the plural form of *wolf*

4. to sing without words

5. Your mother's sister is your ___.

7. homonym of *plain* (a jet)

10. homonym of *or* (you row with it)

12. compound word meaning past 12 P.M. but before 6 P.M.

15. shortened form of *gasoline*

16. prefix in the word *rethink*

17. homonym of *in* (a place to stay)

18. another homonym of clue #10 ACROSS (a metal)

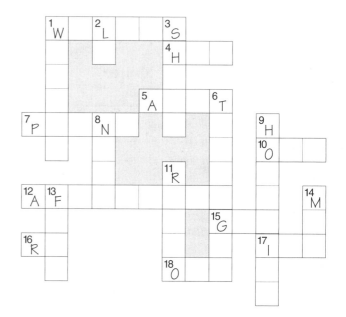

DOWN

1. *Rabbit* is to *hop* as *duck* is to ___.

2. suffix in the word *perfectly*

3. antonym of *whisper*

6. a three-sided figure

8. slang word meaning *no*

9. compound word meaning "lonesome for one's home"

11. cowboy contest

13. homonym of *feat* (plural form of *foot*)

14. abbreviation for *Monday*

Name: _____   Date: _____

SCOPE & SEQUENCE

STUDENT	Definitions	Synonyms	Multiple-Meaning Words	Antonyms	Base Words	Prefixes	Suffixes	Compound Words	Contractions	Possessives	Homonyms	Confusing Words	Rhyming Words	Shortened Words	Idioms	Vivid Words	Parts of Speech	Alphabetical Order	Guide Words	Syllables

SCOPE & SEQUENCE

STUDENT	Pronunciation	Definitions	Spelling	Irregular Plurals	Slang	Connotations	Euphemisms	Analogies	Abbreviations	Foreign Words	Names	Figures of Speech	Word Origins	Word Roots	History/Government Words	Geography/People & Cultures Words	Science/Weather Words	Media/Marketplace Words	Health/Sports Words	Music/Restaurant Words

PAGE 6
1. T 4. T 7. T
2. T 5. F
3. T 6. T

PAGE 7
1. knob 4. hum
2. hero 5. dozen
3. chore

PAGE 8
1. raw 7. nearly
2. ache 8. pal
3. exchange 9. journal
4. shore 10. cellar
5. usually 11. hidden
6. pupils 12. rim

PAGE 9
A. 1. gift 3. guard
   2. give 4. glad
B. 1. part 3. package
   2. pit 4. pig

PAGE 10
1. stroll 5. pup
2. frosty 6. powerful
3. ivory 7. eager
4. replied

PAGE 11
1. stroll 5. witness
2. ivory 6. frosty
3. exchange 7. hum
4. journal
SOLUTION: *synonym*

PAGE 12
1. Rarely 6. neighboring
2. usually 7. beside
3. promptly 8. distant
4. never 9. among
5. Always 10. inside

PAGE 13
Sentences will vary but should include the "when" and "where" words listed at the top of the page.

PAGE 14
Pictures will vary.

PAGE 15
1. a, d 3. a, b
2. b, c 4. b, d
Challenge: scale

PAGE 16
1. coast 4. ground
2. set 5. boxed
3. gear

PAGE 17
1. tie 4. match
2. fly 5. case
3. drawing

PAGE 18
1. bat 5. box
2. story 6. current
3. bat 7. current
4. box 8. story

PAGE 19
Answers will vary.

PAGE 20
1. b 4. c 7. b
2. c 5. a 8. d
3. a 6. d

PAGE 21
1. cold 5. child
2. far 6. bold
3. wise 7. worst
4. past 8. healthy

PAGE 22
A. 1. A 5. A 9. S
   2. A 6. A 10. A
   3. S 7. A
   4. S 8. S
B. 1. yelled *or* 5. scared *or*
      shouted frightened
   2. moist *or* 6. repair
      damp 7. admit
   3. clumsy 8. center
   4. straight

PAGE 23
1. trip 6. blind
2. crowd 7. ditch
3. test 8. dusk
4. sand 9. fear
5. begged 10. bravery

PAGE 24
1. lively 5. exit
2. polite 6. public
3. stale 7. shallow
4. arose

PAGE 25
1. c 3. a 5. b
2. a 4. c 6. c

PAGE 26
1. codlinks, c
2. grawp, b
3. klampliver, a
4. fledlamk, c
5. fizmark, b
6. lorghat, a
7. qualtzmk, c
8. wraxbuldman, c

PAGE 27
1. buy 2. someone who buys something
3. something that doesn't work or do what it's supposed to 4. say that something is wrong
5. money given back
6. to trade one thing for something else
7. people who sell things
8. angry; mad

PAGE 28
A. 1. twilight 5. polite
   2. merchant 6. courage
   3. exit 7. shallow
   4. arose 8. stale
B. Sentences will vary.

PAGE 29
A. 1. straight 6. home
   2. open 7. cook
   3. new 8. spell
   4. take 9. zip
   5. low 10. appear
B. 1. longer, longing
   2. payment, repay
   3. freedom, freely
   4. kindly, unkind
   5. hurtful, hurting
   6. hummed, humming
   7. doing, redo
   8. smiling, smiles

PAGE 30
A. 1. work 13. America
   2. surprise 14. fool
   3. use 15. hunt
   4. slight 16. dance
   5. ask 17. ease
   6. near 18. win
   7. make 19. soon
   8. happy 20. fat
   9. hope 21. magic
   10. grasp 22. force
   11. tie 23. wealth
   12. search 24. drift
B. 1. drift 3. America
   2. magic

PAGE 31
1. base word: attract
   a. attraction
   b. attracting
   c. attractive
2. base word: invent
   a. inventor b. invented
   c. invention
3. base word: think
   a. rethink
   b. unthinkable
   c. thinking
4. base word: place
   a. replace
   b. placement
   c. placed

PAGE 32
1. love 4. fortune
2. howl 5. circle
3. farm

PAGE 33
A. 1. un- 6. semi-
   2. pre- 7. fore-
   3. re- 8. super-
   4. dis- 9. mis-
   5. bi- 10. post-
B. 1. disappear
   2. unhealthy
   3. undress
   4. superstar
   5. preteen

PAGE 34
A. 1. reread
   2. redo
   3. reapply

B. 1. superhuman
   2. superpower
   3. superhighway
C. 1. unkind
   2. unlucky
   3. unimportant

PAGE 35
1. untrue
2. retake
3. superman
4. superfine
5. unsafe
6. unwrapped
7. readjust
8. rewash
9. rewrite
10. supermarket

PAGE 36
Circle: unhappy, unkind, unfriendly, unsatisfactory, unfair, unimportant, unlucky
New Paragraph: Margo was happy with her school. The teachers, she felt, were quite kind. The students were friendly. Margo got satisfactory grades, and she felt the grading system was fair. The school staff treated Margo as if she were a very important person. She felt like a most lucky girl, indeed.

PAGE 37
A. 1. -ly 5. -ment 9. -ing
   2. -er 6. -ish 10. -er
   3. -ful 7. -ion
   4. -less 8. -ist
B. 1. honestly
   2. pianist
   3. baker
   4. peaceful
   5. useless

PAGE 38
Sentences will vary.

PAGE 39
1. actor 6. singer
2. artist 7. teacher
3. inventor 8. puppeteer
4. scientist 9. conductor
5. miner 10. engineer

PAGE 40
ACROSS
1. ful 7. actor
3. super 9. hopeless
DOWN
2. use 6. ease
3. surprise 8. redo
4. artist 10. eer
5. unhappy

PAGE 41
1. baseball
2. playground
3. classroom
4. classmates
5. everywhere
6. without
7. upstairs
8. bedroom
9. afternoon
10. raindrops
11. inside

PAGE 42
A. rainbow, homesick, touchdown, snowmobile, anything
B. 1. rainbow
2. touchdown
3. homesick
4. snowmobile
5. anything

PAGE 43
1. football
2. firewood
3. sunset
4. hallway
5. daybreak
6. footprints

PAGE 44
A. 1. birdbath
2. afternoon
3. paintbrush
4. football, baseball, or basketball
B. Answers will vary.

PAGE 45
A. 2. would not
3. you will
4. she is
5. did not
6. I have
7. there is
8. we are
9. I am
10. let us
B. 2. you've
3. here's
4. he'd
5. who's
6. I'd
7. that's
8. wouldn't
9. where's
10. weren't

PAGE 46
A. 1. shouldn't
2. There's
3. it'll
4. she'll
5. didn't
6. might've
B. 1. What is
2. Do not
3. you have
4. You will
5. I am
6. should not

PAGE 47
A. 1. hound's
2. animal's
3. beagle's
4. hunter's
5. greyhound's
6. world's

B. 1. dog's
2. bird's
3. car's
4. girl's

PAGE 48
A. 1. schools' teams
2. clowns' routines
3. bells' ringing
4. members' robes
5. mosquitoes' hum
B. 1. children's
2. oxen's
3. mice's
4. geese's

PAGE 49
A. Possible compound words:
seasick, homesick, seashore, shoreline, airplane, seaplane, airsick, seaside, outside, outline
B. Compound words: cannot, inside
Contractions: couldn't, he's, what's
Possessives: men's, Julia's
Sentences will vary.

PAGE 50
1. hot, hoot
2. son, soon
3. bet, beet
4. slop, sloop
5. ten, teen
6. ad, add
7. put, putt
8. hoping, hopping

PAGE 51
A. 1. need
2. made
3. for
4. too
5. buy
6. great, steak
B. 1. bin
2. hare
3. pare or pear
4. doe
Sentences will vary.

PAGE 52
1. a. whole b. hole
2. a. principle b. principal
3. a. flea b. flee
4. a. plain b. plane
5. a. sleigh b. slay
6. a. reign b. rain
7. a. thrown b. throne

PAGE 53
1. desert
2. weather
3. lose
4. its
5. quite
6. whole
7. quit
8. except
9. die
10. close
Challenge answer: cacti

PAGE 54
1. a. presence b. presents
2. a. chose b. choose
3. a. lead b. led
4. a. advice b. advise
5. a. past b. passed
6. a. lose b. loose

PAGE 55
1. need
2. choose
3. made
4. whole
5. buy
6. great
7. steak
8. dessert
9. super
10. accept

PAGE 56
1. a. cane b. can
2. a. band b. bad
3. a. plant b. plan
4. a. time b. tie
5. a. rabbit b. rabbi
6. a. stole b. sole
7. a. drain b. rain
8. a. draw b. raw
9. a. pint b. pin

PAGE 57
1. bouquet
2. drought
3. awl
4. cousin
5. plummet
6. agile
7. grumpy

PAGE 58
A. 1. photo
2. math
3. ad
4. pop
5. phone
6. gas
7. mike
8. plane
9. prof
10. sub
B. Circle: prof, mike, plane, pop, math, pro, photo

PAGE 59
1. b
2. b
3. a
4. b
5. a

PAGE 60
1. Two heads are better than one.
2. in hot water
3. getting a taste of your own medicine
4. Don't cry over spilled milk.
5. turn over a new leaf

PAGE 61
A. 1. waddled
2. babbled
3. skyscraper
4. mansion
5. toddler
6. china
B. Sentences will vary.

PAGE 62
A. Circle: clank, purred, squealed, buzz, pitter-patter, swish, creak, clink, screech
B. Sentences will vary.

PAGE 63
A. 1. spaniel
2. teens
3. breakfast
4. icy
5. hospital
6. exclaimed
7. generous
8. tasty
B. Answers will vary.

PAGE 64
Sentences will vary.

PAGE 65
1. waddle
2. buzz
3. toddler
4. exclaim
5. mansion
6. boom
7. honk
8. skyscraper

PAGE 66
1. a. noun b. adjective
2. a. noun b. verb
3. a. verb b. noun
4. a. verb b. noun
5. a. noun b. adjective
6. a. noun b. verb
7. a. verb b. noun
8. a. noun b. verb

PAGE 67
2. dance, verb
3. drive, verb
4. drive, noun
5. reward, verb
6. reward, noun
7. blanket, noun
8. blanket, verb
9. joke, verb
10. joke, noun

PAGE 68
1. verb
2. noun
3. verb
4. verb
5. noun
6. adjective
7. noun
8. noun

PAGE 69
Sentences will vary.

PAGE 70
1. noun
2. verb
3. adjective
4. verb
5. noun
6. adjective
7. verb
8. noun
9. noun
10. verb

PAGE 71
1. b
2. a
3. c
4. b
5. a
6. a
7. b
8. c

PAGE 72
A. 1. joyfully
2. comfortably
3. richly
4. tearfully
5. angrily
6. perfectly
B. Sentences will vary.

PAGE 73
1. cab
2. rob
3. lab
4. bay
5. ray
6. coal
7. royal
8. cob
9. vocal
10. vary

PAGE 74
Sentences will vary.

PAGE 75
A. 1. happiness
2. suggest
3. bold
4. ballet
5. doll
6. business
7. flea
8. parachute
B. ample, answer, apple, brain, breakfast, famous, foreign, forward, globe, key, reason, religion, thick, thin, vacation

PAGE 76
A. 1. nor, nope, normal
2. quest, question
3. spell, spend
4. zip, zoo, zone
B. Answers will vary.

PAGE 77
A. 1. 135
2. 123
3. 130
4. 123
5. 135
6. 135
7. 130
8. 123
9. 130
10. 135
B. Sentences will vary.

PAGE 78
1. ath•lete
2. soc•cer
3. gym•na•si•um
4. sta•di•um
5. court
6. a•re•na
7. O•lym•pics
8. tro•phy
9. track
10. tour•na•ment
11. cham•pi•on
12. ex•er•cise
13. hock•ey
14. race
15. re•lay
16. vic•to•ry

PAGE 79
A. view, route, trip, train, inn, gate, fare, price, map, flight, guide

B. 1. va•ca•tion
2. re•ser•va•tion
3. tour•ist
4. sum•mer
5. de•par•ture
6. tick•et
7. fare•well
8. re•cre•a•tion
9. ho•tel
10. air•port
11. des•ti•na•tion
12. back•pack
13. jour•ney
14. sou•ve•nir

PAGE 80
A. 1. b   3. b   5. a
2. a   4. b   6. a
B. 2. glor´ y
3. met´ al
4. con demn´
5. gey´ ser
6. ex´ tra
7. met´ e or
8. rain´ storm
9. de clare´
10. un clean´
11. re ply´
12. muz´ zle

PAGE 81
1. 1   4. 1   7. 2
2. 2   5. 1   8. 1
3. 2   6. 2   9. 3

PAGE 82
1. a   3. c   5. c
2. c   4. a

PAGE 83
1. to touch with the fingers *or* to play a musical instrument by using certain fingers on the strings of keys
2. adj.; hot and damp with little movement of air
3. yes; to follow or hunt like a dog
4. no
5. not able to see
6. a window shade with slats

PAGE 84
1. showing information by a row of numbers rather than on a dial
2. moved in a bumpy, jerky manner
3. a deep red color
4. quickly, in a very short time
5. a person who saves or rescues
6. like or suggesting metal

PAGE 85
A. Checks should be by #1, 3, 5, 6, 8, 9, 11, and 13. The letter C should be by #2, 4, 7, 10, 12, 14, and 15.
Correct spelling of checked words:
1. balloons
3. government
5. hammock
6. photograph
8. bucket
9. pioneer
11. backwards
13. villain
B. Sentences will vary.

PAGE 86
1. cris´   3. yes
2. adjective   4. yes
5. a pigeon-like bird
6. en•ter•tain   7. yes
8. a small, long-armed ape of southeast Asia
9. sax•o•phone
10. answer depends on the dictionary used
11. poorly done or made
12. yes

PAGE 87
A. 1. T   4. F   7. T
2. T   5. T   8. T
3. F   6. T
B. Sentences will vary.

PAGE 88
1. bail
2. mow
3. males
4. peek
5. tax
6. haunt
7. batter
8. draft
9. snores

PAGE 89
1. fast; meaning big
2. quick; directions
3. hotel; school subjects
4. toddler; relatives
5. desert; related to the beach
6. jet; types of ground vehicles
7. shelter; weather conditions
8. basket; related to baseball
9. repaired; meaning broken
10. dictionary; verbs or action words

PAGE 90
A. 1. teeth   3. people
2. shelves   4. wolves
B. 1. calves   4. thieves
2. knives   5. feet
3. mice
Sentences will vary.

PAGE 91
1. wives
2. lives
3. loaves
4. scarves
5. halves
6. leaves
7. women
8. cacti
9. oxen
10. elves

PAGE 92
A. 1. b   5. g   9. c
2. f   6. h   10. a
3. e   7. d
4. i   8. j
B. Slang words and sentences will vary.

PAGE 93
A. 1. gentleman   7. thrifty
2. request   8. complain
3. cautious   9. amusing
4. unusual   10. duties
5. curious   11. daring
6. heavy   12. work
B. Sentences will vary.

PAGE 94
A. 1. –   3. –   5. +
2. +   4. +   6. –
B. 1. Easygoing Ernie
2. Carefree Carla
3. Unique Monique
4. Natural Nellie
5. Naughty Nicky

PAGE 95
A. 1. pass away
2. visually impaired
3. intelligence agent
4. beef
5. memorial service
6. hairstylist
7. golden years
8. pre-owned vehicle
B. 2. jail or prison
3. poor student
4. unemployed

PAGE 96
A. 1. d   4. c   7. e
2. f   5. g   8. b
3. h   6. a
B. 1. I was sorry to hear that Mrs. Watson's husband died.
2. All public buildings should have an entrance for crippled people.
3. Lester Lee was hired as a janitor.

PAGE 97
A. 1. a   3. c
2. b   4. b
B. Sentences will vary.

PAGE 98
1. sad
2. lemon
3. hungry
4. junior
5. cage
6. walk
7. glove
8. pilot
9. green
10. date

PAGE 99
1. twelve 6. patch
2. fork 7. vegetable
3. dull 8. zoo
4. eye 9. moisten
5. fawn 10. Canyon

PAGE 100
ACROSS: 2. hot 5. kitten
6. finger 7. today
9. year 11. ten
DOWN: 1. shoe 3. moon
4. library 8. oar
10. eat

PAGE 101
1. Bachelor of Arts
2. District Attorney
3. each 4. January
5. Food and Drug Administration
6. Company 7. Senior
8. Monday
9. as soon as possible
10. tablespoon

PAGE 102
1. Nov.; November
2. Dr.; Doctor
3. Capt.; Captain
4. NBC; National Broadcasting Company
5. D.C.; District of Columbia
6. IRS; Internal Revenue Service
7. FBI; Federal Bureau of Investigation

PAGE 103
Captions will vary. Be sure two workout words are used in each sentence.

PAGE 104
1. b 3. a 5. b
2. b 4. a 6. a

PAGE 105
A. 1. e 3. d 5. b
2. a 4. c
B. Sentences will vary.

PAGE 106
A. 1. aunt
2. uncle
3. father-in-law
4. cousin
5. great-grandmother
6. stepfather
7. stepbrother
8. spouse
B. 1. stepbrother
2. nephew
3. siblings
4. sister-in-law
5. great-grandfather

PAGE 107
A. 1. dad 7. none
2. uncle 8. uncle
3. none dad
4. none cousin
5. cousin aunt
6. none
B. Sentences will vary.

PAGE 108
A. Smell: a gas leak, perfume; Hear: a doorbell, a melody; Taste: some sugar, salt; See: a photograph, a rainbow; Feel: a warm breeze, a burn
B. 1. taste 7. taste
2. smell 8. touch
3. smell 9. sight
4. sight 10. touch
5. hearing 11. hearing
6. touch 12. taste

PAGE 109
1. pickle, sweet, sour
2. makes, wailing, screeching
3. harm, warm, bright
4. hot, bubbling, hot
5. score, stomped, roar

PAGE 110
A. & B. Sentences will vary.

PAGE 111
A. 1. d 3. c 5. a
2. e 4. b
B. 1. b 3. a
2. b 4. a

PAGE 112
A. 1. rain, welcome stranger
2. light, blood
3. body, machine
4. Saturday, best friend
5. purse, banana
6. problem, weight
7. smile, rainbow
8. candy bar, mud puddle
9. rumor, flu
10. dancers, wildflowers
B. Likely answers:
1. kangaroos
2. diamonds
3. bees or ants
4. ox
5. clacking typewriter keys
Students may have made up their own answers.

PAGE 113
1. wind - furnace
2. pavement - stove top
3. paint color - coffee with cream
4. sweat - waterfall
5. paint job - A+ test score
6. ice cubes - bells
7. sunburned face - strawberry ice cream cone

PAGE 114
A. 1. automobile 4. market
2. bus 5. proud
3. neighbor 6. out
B. 1. named after Roman emperor Julius Caesar
2. named after England's Earl of Sandwich
3. named after Mars, the Roman god of war
4. from an Old English word meaning "the moon's day"

PAGE 115

```
            B
 G (A Q U A R I U M)
 E           C     E
 O       T   Y     N
 G       R   C     O
 R (T R I A N G L E)H
 A       P   E     P
 P     (L A U N N A)E
 H       E         L
 Y     (T R I O)   E
(N O I S I V E L E T)
(A N N I V E R S A R Y)
```

PAGE 116
1. aquarium
2. bicycle
3. triangle
4. triplets
5. trio
6. telephone
7. television
8. geography
9. annual
10. anniversary

PAGE 117
A. 1. b 3. d 5. c
2. f 4. a 6. e
B. century, dictator, colony, revolution, decade, civil war

PAGE 118
A. 1. c 4. b 7. e
2. g 5. f
3. a 6. d
B. Candidate, citizens, election, vote, campaign, ballot, constitution

PAGE 119
A. 1. f 3. e 5. b
2. c 4. a 6. d
B. globe, border, coast, port, population, climate

PAGE 120
A. 1. c 3. b 5. a
2. f 4. d 6. e
B. immigrants, custom, religion, ancestors, legends, artifacts

PAGE 121
1. immigrants
2. revolution
3. legend
4. artifacts
5. border
6. population
7. ballot
8. coast
9. climate
10. port

PAGE 122
A. 1. species 4. mammal
2. cell 5. behave
3. skeleton 6. prey
B. 1. skeleton 4. cells
2. prey 5. species
3. mammals

PAGE 123
A. 1. volcano 4. smog
2. glacier 5. erode
3. fault
B. 1. volcano 4. losing
2. fall in it ground
3. forest fire 5. glaciers

PAGE 124
DOWN: 1. forecast
ACROSS: 1. fog 2. cloud
3. degrees 4. hail
5. humidity

PAGE 125
A. 1. d 4. a 7. f
2. c 5. g
3. e 6. b
B. 1. broadcast
2. editorial
3. headline
4. feature
5. reporter
6. network
7. interview

PAGE 126
1. buying things
2. taken off
3. gives the holder special rights
4. sell
5. the price
6. at a lower-than-usual price

PAGE 127
Paragraphs will vary.

PAGE 128
A. 1. virus
2. contagious
3. exercise
4. diet
5. emergency
6. first aid

B. Sentences will vary.

PAGE 129
Answers and headlines will vary.

PAGE 130
1. score
2. cheer
3. goal
4. team
5. practice
6. field
7. court
8. opponent

PAGE 131
violin, solo, duet, soprano, opera, piano, tempo, trombone, Bravo

PAGE 132
1. used to express approval, especially of a performance
2. two people singing or playing music together
3. a play in which the words are all sung
4. a large musical instrument with a keyboard
5. one person singing or playing music alone
6. the highest kind of singing voice
7. the rate of speed of a musical piece
8. a large, brass horn with a long, bent tube that slides in and out to change the tones
9. a musical instrument having four strings and played with a bow

PAGE 133
1. c   6. b   11. g
2. m   7. e   12. j
3. f   8. d   13. h
4. i   9. k
5. a   10. l

PAGE 134
A. Restaurant reviews will vary.

B. 1. sautéed
2. simmered
3. roasted
4. deep-fried
5. blended
6. grilled
7. poached

PAGE 135
1. request
2. ballet
3. basketball
4. pay
5. mice
6. cousin

7. married to
8. three
9. neigh´ (first)
10. November
11. super
12. Sunday
13. glad
14. noun
15. happy
16. shouldn't
17. sloop
18. hear it

PAGE 136
ACROSS: 1. wolves   4. hum
5. aunt   7. plane
10. oar   12. afternoon
15. gas   16. re   17. inn
18. ore
DOWN: 1. waddle   2. ly
3. shout   6. triangle
8. nope   9. homesick
11. rodeo   13. feet
14. Mon.